"Midge is a hilarious satirical essayist and nonfiction writer, and her work brings all the laughs. But they are 'thinky' laughs, because the humor doubles back on itself and makes you see so much about modern Native American life in a new way."
—David Treuer, *Los Angeles Times*

"This uproarious, truth-telling collection of satirical essays skewer[s] everything from white feminism to 'Pretendians' to pumpkin spice. Midge, a member of the Standing Rock Sioux Tribe, muses bitingly on life as a Native woman in America, staring colonialism and racism in the face wherever she finds them, from offensive Halloween costumes to exploitative language. This collection's deliciously sharp edges draw laughter and blood alike."
—Adrienne Westenfeld, *Esquire*

"Midge is a wry, astute charmer with an eye for detail and an ear for the scruffy rhythms of American lingo."
—Sarah Vowell, author of
Lafayette in the Somewhat United States

"[Midge's] no-b.s., take-no-prisoners approach is likely to resound with twenty-something readers, but the older crowd ought to give Midge a look, too."
—Joan Curbow, *Booklist*

"[A] cornucopia of literary brilliance. The Standing Rock Sioux writer's wickedly funny autobiography offers laugh-out-loud passages alongside compassionate profiles, bitter sarcasm, and heartbreaking chronicles. . . . Every entry is so well-crafted that the only disappointment you'll find is when you realize you've read them all. Then again, this is a book that demands to be reread."
—Ryan Winn, *Tribal College Journal of
American Indian Higher Education*

"Abundant with brilliant satire."
—*Shelf Awareness*

"This collection of opinion editorials and recent essays solidifies Midge's standing as one of the most versatile talents in Native and American writing today."
—Samantha Majhor,
American Indian Culture and Research Journal

"If you're wondering why the presence of Andrew Jackson's portrait in the Oval Office is offensive, this is your book."

—*Kirkus Reviews*

"*Bury My Heart at Chuck E. Cheese's* is timely reading for the fall season, with Midge suggesting 'Politically Correct Alternatives to Culturally Insensitive Halloween Costumes,' and proclaiming 'Hey America, I'm Taking Back Thanksgiving.' Treat yourself to a fast-moving correction of any vestiges you may have of the stoic, unsmiling Native stereotype and enjoy at least a tweet or a one-liner from Tiffany Midge. You're sure to learn something as you laugh."

—Jan Hardy, *Back in the Stacks*

"Tiffany Midge is the kind of funny that can make the same joke funny over and over again. Which means, of course, that she is wicked smart, and sly, and that she has her hand on the pulse of the culture in a Roxane Gay-ish way, only funnier, and that she has our number, your number, and my number too, all of our numbers. Which means she is our teacher, if we let her be."

—Pam Houston, author of *Deep Creek: Finding Hope in the High Country*

"Tiffany Midge is a gift, a literary comedic genius. *Bury My Heart at Chuck E. Cheese's* is chock-full of savagely clever and spot-on riffs about Native life combined with keen observations of the absurdities of pop culture. Where else can one find discussion of the use of 'ugh' in American literature or of Anne Coulter and Dolores Abernathy as judges in the post-election U.S. Open in Racist Tirades Competition? Adroit, snarly, essential, and inspiring. She knows our truths, so there is no use in hiding. Midge is among the very best Indigenous writers. More, please."

—Devon Mihesuah, author of *Ned Christie, Choctaw Crime and Punishment,* and *Indigenous American Women*

The Dreamcatcher in the Wry

Tiffany Midge

INTRODUCTION BY DEVON A. MIHESUAH

University of Nebraska Press
Lincoln

Acknowledgments for the use of
copyrighted material appear on pages
211–12, which constitute an extension
of the copyright page.

The University of Nebraska Press is part of a
land-grant institution with campuses and programs
on the past, present, and future homelands of the
Pawnee, Ponca, Otoe-Missouria, Omaha, Dakota,
Lakota, Kaw, Cheyenne, and Arapaho Peoples,
as well as those of the relocated Ho-Chunk,
Sac and Fox, and Iowa Peoples.

Library of Congress
Cataloging-in-Publication Data
Names: Midge, Tiffany, 1965– author. |
Mihesuah, Devon A., 1957– writer of introduction.
Title: The dreamcatcher in the wry / Tiffany Midge;
introduction by Devon A. Mihesuah.
Description: Lincoln: University of Nebraska Press, 2024.
Identifiers: LCCN 2024023899
ISBN 9781496240149 (hardback)
ISBN 9781496242129 (epub)
ISBN 9781496242136 (pdf)
Subjects: LCSH: Indian women authors—Anecdotes. |
American literature—Indian authors. | Indian wit and humor. |
BISAC: HUMOR / Form / Essays |
BIOGRAPHY & AUTOBIOGRAPHY / Women | LCGFT: Essays. | Humor.
Classification: LCC PS3613.I3628 D74 2024 |
DDC 814/.6 [B]—dc23/eng/20240618
LC record available at https://lccn.loc.
gov/2024023899

Designed and set in Fournier MT Pro by Lacey Losh.

Dedicated to my mother

This one time when I was a girl I was hanging out at the Tastee Freez with Patsy and Johnnie Poopsack. We were chattering away and gossiping about every person who happened to be walking by. In a sudden flash of moral introspection Johnnie pointed out that we were acting mean and petty and that we should stop badmouthing everybody. So just like that, all our chatter and fun came to an abrupt stop and we just sat in utter silence for a long, long time with nothing at all to say.

–Alita Smith (my mom)

Some people choose radical love.
I choose incredulity and radical sarcasm.

–TMidge

Hey dude, can you not have your spirit animal hump my leg.
Thanks.

—Trevino Brings Plenty

Contents

Foreword

DEVON MIHESUAH

Wit may be a thing of pure imagination,
but humor involves sentiment and character.
—Henry Giles

When I was asked to write the forward to Tiffany Midge's enviable collection of writings, I was not sure I could do it. I'm not a best-selling author and I'm not particularly funny. I do understand and appreciate humor, however, and not only is Tiffany one of my favorite writers, she is one of my favorite people.

As a historian who focuses on Native history and cultures, I necessarily study the causes and effects of colonization and racism. These issues are difficult enough to teach and publish about, but most Natives also have stories about atrocities that affect our families and communities. If we are not enduring trauma, we often spend too much time thinking about how to avoid it. Composing stories with happy endings is one way to alleviate stress.

Tiffany asks: "Can I even claim being Native if I don't have a personal trauma narrative replete with a strong message of hope and redemption?" This question pretty much sums up the state of Native writings today. Many popular fiction writers focus on our horrifying histories and current challenging realities. And those offerings seem to be what readers expect about Natives.

The reality, however, is that Native people are not wallowing in misery 24/7, but non-Natives don't know that. Tiffany Midge might be a literary comedian but make no mistake—she knows what Native peoples face. She does not consider "Indian humor" an "antidote" to the plethora of intergenerational trauma tales. She explains that humor and joy are "fundamental values encompassing the human experience." I recall that after *Custer Died for Your Sins* was published, someone called Vine Deloria Jr. a "savage wit." That struck me as racist, but also an odd thing to say because Native people have always had wicked senses of humor. What Natives find funny might not always be clear to those who do not spend time around them, but laughter is an integral part of Native reality.

And that need for laughter is reflected in this collection. Tiffany wields her gifts of perception and creativity to mesh the positive, the negative, and the absurd found in the daily social, political, economic, and religious issues that affect all of us. She deftly addresses organ transplants, political correctness, hibernating bears, COVID, her super-powered uterus, organ meat as love offerings, bison bladder whoopee cushions, Auntie B's beadwork erotica, buckskin romances, the popularity of stereotypical novels about Indians written by non-Natives *and* Natives who have figured out what side of the marketable fry bread to butter, and, of course, *The Field Guide to Native American Women of the Southwest*.

Tiffany says, "Critical awareness is just the first step toward repairing, restoration, and reconciliation." She offers us relief with her wry observations and, ironically, the uncomfortable truths. Her honest musings pull us in, engage us, and inspire us.

Devon Mihesuah, an enrolled citizen of the Choctaw Nation of Oklahoma, is the Cora Lee Beers Price Professor in the Hall Center for the Humanities at the University of Kansas.

THE DREAMCATCHER IN THE WRY

1

Moscow/Pullman Daily News Columns

1

The Dreamcatcher in the Wry

Occasionally, Jon, my partner, will rescue various kinds of items abandoned on the sorting table at the post office. Or in the dental office. Or on the street. He brings the various odds and ends home, these found objects or trinkets, and imagines some future repurposing, some further use, a key with the potential to unlock efficiency and thrift. Last week it was a decorative dreamcatcher made in China. I smirked at its cellophane wrap, its implausible magic, before chucking it into the bin. And then a couple of days later I found the dreamcatcher lying out again. "Back into the bin with you," I thought. Later, Jon noticed it tossed out like yesterday's birdcage liner. "Why are you throwing out a perfectly good dreamcatcher?" He thought it deserved to be hung up somewhere in the house or given away.

"I can't expend the energy required in deciding what to do with it," I explained. "I already have enough stuff in the house to fill a semitruck. Besides, it's janky, appropriative, and would probably give off bad medicine." Dreamcatchers. They don't hold any allure for me, not when they're commonly sold at truck stops next to MAGA hats and Slim Jims. One year Jon made some out of yarn and coat hangers and attached miniature Hula dancers and wishbones to them. I don't know if I convinced him. The dreamcatcher is still somewhere in the house, its glittery feathers, copper threads, and turquoise pony beads waiting for someone to offer amnesty or give clemency.

Need a homemade bookmark? We have a pile of them. Looking for an animated bass that mounts to the wall and sings "Take Me to the River?" I got you covered. What about a plastic bonsai tree? I have one of those. I have dozens of gallon milk jugs. Rows of avocado pits trying to flower in the windowsill, every kind of glass jar known to mankind, piles of yogurt containers, stacks of paper, a cupboard with nothing but old to-go coffee containers, and a tiny pair of men's oxfords found at the local swimming pool. And don't get me started on my stuff. Books, magazines, clothing, art supplies, ephemera for making collages, photo albums, linens, old typewriters galore. One man's trash is another man's treasure goes the adage. I have no rubric for measuring the stuff I stash into piles or drawers or boxes, since my tastes are entirely subjective, as are his. This is what I try to remind myself.

This week Jon put together five-shelf metal storage racks. Four of them. They are voluminous and impressive. They're to be tasked with getting our storage boxes off the floor, our this and thats, flotsam and jetsam, and will initiate a sense of ease and order. Now that the stuff is on view, I can easily ascertain what needs to be thrown away, what's expendable, and what's worth keeping.

In the meantime, there are zucchinis in our dining area the size of my thighs. Are we supposed to eat them or challenge them to a duel? Jon found them on the church's take-away table. He insists we save seeds from any produce we've procured. I've designated an area in the kitchen to store seeds. We are not doomsday preppers, we're not even gardeners, but some low-grade facsimile of them. You could say that one man's doomsday is another man's nightmare. Good thing we have one of those dreamcatchers to filter out the nightmares. That is if it didn't get thrown out.

2

I'm Not a Cat

America's Funniest Housecat Videos

If the pandemic could be described in one perfectly absurd soundbite, it would be when Texas lawyer Rod Ponton appeared before Judge Roy Ferguson's virtual Judicial District Court in Texas as an adorable little cat. It was a "faux paw" viewed around the world. Is Ponton actually a cat? "Catsolutely" not. Somehow the Zoom filter on his secretary's computer was set on "cat."

When I first saw the "catastrophe," I laughed so hard it induced a coughing fit. I laughed (and coughed) so hard Jon came running down the hall from the other room. "What's the matter? Are you okay?" He found me gagging for breath on the bed, red in the face, trying not to wet my pants. The second I recovered I showed him the video on my phone. He laughed and laughed hard, but his lungs are better than mine, so there wasn't concern that he might go into "catdiac" arrest.

The Late Late Show with James Corden suggested show titles if the cat lawyer premise was optioned for TV: "Furry Friday," "The Furry DA," "Clawyers," "The Cat's Meow," or my favorite: "Claw and Order." "Cat Lawyer" would be a shoo-in for a TV series or Disney movie. I grew up on episodes of *Bewitched*, where Endora was perpetually transforming her son-in-law into this and that—a pony, a werewolf, a toad, a billy goat. The idea of shape-shifting is old hat for me. Native American creation stories and legends are full of all kinds of shape-shifters. I was convinced my grandpa could be in two places at the same time and that my mother shifted into a bird after she died. So, when a lawyer shows up in virtual court as a cat, maybe it's not a Zoom filter. Maybe he really is a cat, despite his plea to the contrary: "I'm here live. I'm not a cat."

Sometime last year, my partner, Jon, left me to go housesit a friend's four cats. For one week I indulged in A: Solitude. B: The toilet lid being put down where Goddess intended it should be. And C: Splaying my limbs out on the bed like a starfish. Ah, the novelty of having the house to myself after weeks of nonstop "togetherness," after weeks of quarantine. The "solitude" was short-lived, however, because within an hour Jon messaged me the first dispatch of what was to become the cats' videography. For the rest of the week, I received one cat video after another. But who could blame him? The cats were as irresistible as runway models—pouty, enigmatic, replete with "a smokey eye." The cats also bore names that were similar to runway models—Tia, Gadget, Nutmeg, and Cricket.

Among his responsibilities, Jon was tasked with herding them all inside before dark for inventory, rather "fur-ventory," or "feline-tory." Usually they came willingly, but once or twice Jon had to search for them in the yard with a flashlight and cat treats. "Ah, a cat whisperer," I texted back at him. "You have your work cut out for you, good luck." He has a special way with cats; he says he speaks their language. He often speaks "Cat" with me, meowing whenever he enters a room, for instance. Meowing when he wants to excuse himself. Anything more advanced than that and I don't understand. I'm not fluent in Cat.

I don't understand a lot of things that he easily understands, so I consult with him often. One night I was reading an article out loud to him while he was drifting off to sleep. The article discussed how Western literature's origins derive from theological texts. The article mentioned Calvin. I asked Jon if he'd read Calvin, and in a half-asleep state he said, "You mean Calvin and Hobbes?"

Every few weeks, Jon asks me if we should adopt a cat. "Should we get a cat?"

"Sure," I tell him. "I'd like to have Siamese cats, but like, conjoined."

Our landlords don't allow cats, but we get the sense they could be persuaded. "I'll make them an offer they "cat'nt" refuse," Jon says as if he's a cat godfather, in addition to a cat sitter, a cat whisperer, and a fluent Cat speaker: "Cat as a Second Language, CSL." CSL fluency would sure come in handy for the cat lawyer. I've watched that video about a hundred times now, and it never gets old.

3

What's Schadenfreude Got to Do with It?

We see it in the news every summer: tourists who don't think the rules apply to them. Every summer, in our national parks, without fail, some poor sap seeking to commune with nature will approach a bison, reach out and actually try to pet it, and end up getting tossed like a Caesar salad. Most people have sense enough to avoid wandering across four lanes of traffic during rush hour, so you'd think approaching a two-thousand-pound bull with massive horns might be regarded as a similarly hazardous situation. Nope. Apparently not.

Most of the Native folks that I know tend to regard these incidents with a little bit of schadenfreude. And that's because bison took such good care of our people, our ancestors, and we feel an affinity for bison and also feel protective toward them. Bison are our relatives. And like us, they were hunted nearly to extinction. If I knew the Lakota word for schadenfreude, I would cite that. "Schadenfreude," in case you're not aware, is a German word that means "pleasure derived from other people's misfortune." From "schaden," meaning damage or harm, and "freude," meaning joy or pleasure: damage-joy.

According to the book *Schadenfreude* by Tiffany Watt Smith, cultures all over the world have similar definitions for the experience of taking pleasure in others' misfortunes. Especially for those who seem deserving of the misfortune. Smith writes that the Japanese have a saying—"the misfortunes of others taste like honey." The Danish speak of "skadefryd," while the Dutch say "leedvermaak." There is a word in Hebrew: "simcha la-ed"—and words in Serbo-Croat, Russian, and Mandarin. The Romans as far back as two thousand years ago spoke of "malevolentia." And the

Greeks had terms for schadenfreude even earlier. All of this is to say that I've been thinking about schadenfreude a lot lately. And not just because tourists have been mistaking Yellowstone National Park for a petting zoo. Mostly, like a lot of other people, I've been horrified by the actions (or inactions) of vaccine deniers—"American patriots" who seem overly cavalier, even proud, about prolonging COVID so the virus infects more and more people, mutates, becomes even more infectious, and burdens our health-care system to the point that unvaccinated people are jeopardizing emergency care for the people who need it. It's like watching a multi-car pileup in slow motion. Earlier in the week, Idaho governor Brad Little asked to bring in 220 health-care workers available through federal programs, and he mobilized 150 Idaho National Guard soldiers to deal with the increase in unvaccinated COVID patients. On Tuesday, Governor Little said only four intensive care beds were available in the entire state of Idaho.

So, when I began to hear the reports about people turning to livestock deworming medication as a preventive or cure for COVID, my sense of schadenfreude took over. When a friend said they weren't feeling the same zest and enjoyment for life they had experienced in better times, I thought about how I've actually *enjoyed* seeing the Trumpsters and vaccine deniers take themselves out with parasite medication. It's life's small pleasures that make life meaningful: the sound of rain, a cat purring in my lap, that first sip of lemony iced tea on a hot summer day, and Trumpsters self-medicating with Ivermectin.

It's beyond appalling that people would rather believe that injecting disinfectant, as Trump reported during a 2020 press briefing, or poisoning themselves with horse de-wormer, is a reasonable alternative to a viably tested and proven vaccine.

Last month COVID-19 cases in South Dakota shot up by more than 450 percent since the start of the annual Sturgis Motorcycle Rally. The rally is just another super-spreader event populated by anti-vax, COVID denying pro-Trumpsters. Schadenfreude, anyone? Yes, please! Ever since rally enthusiasts, a few years ago, planned to build a massive biker bar, campground, and resort compound on Indigenous holy grounds at Matȟó Pahá, or Bear Butte, I've felt more than a little contemptuous toward the rally goers. Paha Sapa, the Black Hills, are sacred to the Indigenous tribes in South Dakota, the Oceti Sakowin Oyate (People of Seven Council Fires), where my mother and grandparents were born, so it is a little more than an affront to have the lands disrespected in all manner of ways, year after year. It's really just the tip of the schadenfreude iceberg.

4

Ramona Quimby Was My Very First Literary Hero

Shy and nonconforming, as a kid I was a hot mess. I never seemed to say or do the right things. And Ramona Quimby taught me that it was okay to be me. The term "a hot mess" hadn't yet arrived in the lexicon during the years I was growing up, but it perfectly described me—likely still does. In the days before diapers for kids were ordinary, I routinely wet my pants, until the day I first set foot inside Mrs. Thompson's Kindergarten classroom and something clicked. I must have realized that getting my shit together was a preferable alternative to risking social disgrace, possibly irrevocably and forever.

What would Ramona Quimby do? wwrqd?

Despite having passed my bladder-control hurdle with flying colors, unfortunately, I continued to wet the bed. Until one summer, during the routine two-week visit at my grandparents', my grandfather suddenly got wise and began setting his alarm for 5:00 a.m. in order to march me, half-asleep, to the bathroom. I don't know why no one had thought of this sooner. It would have saved untold amounts of laundry and shame.

"Laundry and Shame: A Memoir."

In addition to incontinence, I was considered to be resistant to learning and preferred to stare out the window and daydream. My daydreams weren't complicated; they centered around my taking care of baby animals in the animal sanctuary I planned to own one day when I was big enough to take out a line of credit. Or else I daydreamed about a pop idol seeing me on the street or in a restaurant and falling instantly and head over heels in love with me. Or else I daydreamed about being discovered by a talent scout and spectacularly appearing on the *Donny and Marie Show* wearing a purple and silver sequined jumpsuit.

In real life, when I wasn't staring out of windows fantasizing about performing duets of "Proud Mary" with Tina Turner, and making out backstage with both Donny AND Marie, I lagged developmentally behind my peers. I hadn't learned to tie my shoes; all those tricky loops confounded me. This was before Velcro. And I couldn't tell time, either. The concept of a round clockface, hands that went hither-wither, and numbers that corresponded with some temporal comprehension of existence were beyond me. This was in the years before digital clocks. The years before cell phones. In the years before a heart emoji sufficed for a Hallmark sympathy card and a casserole when someone died.

Eventually, I mastered the art of tying my shoes. Obviously. And I figured out how to tell time, for whatever good it has done me because I'm always late. But the struggle and the humiliations with learning these rudimentary and now defunct life skills have never left me. And anxieties around learning still pervade. I can imagine that Ramona Quimby was not without her anxieties and insecurities too. As a child, spending time with Ramona provided comfort and fellowship. Ramona Quimby was many things, and being headstrong, impulsive, and feisty was just the start. She had, of course, many more traits that I could identify with. Many more traits that I could draw strength from. And likely emulate.

When I was in the sixth grade the Especially Special Persons project (ESP) was implemented. ESP was a year-long project, consisting of completing various tasks—akin to earning Scout badges. A student earned an ESP badge and became eligible for privileges like chewing gum, getting soda from the machine in the teachers' lounge, and extended recess. By the end of the year, the fifty plus sixth graders at my school were on board with this process of indoctrination except for me and Ricky, the quiet and shy Mexican boy. Was it remarkable that the only two kids—conscientious objectors—who didn't participate in the program happened to be Native American and Mexican American? I don't know.

But I can tell you that the rest of the students were white. On the last day of school, the ESP kids left the school grounds to go to a nearby park for an unimaginably exciting day of picnic food, games, and prizes. Ricky and I spent the whole afternoon in the classroom, at our desks, like we were being punished in detention. What made an "Especially Special Person" so "Especially Special" if everyone was "Especially Special?" This was a fail as far as I (or Ricky) was concerned.

WWRQD?

Beverly Cleary paved the way for weirdos, laggers, rebels, and hot messes like me.

5

Bitter Homes and Gardens
and Decolonizing My Diet

Spring had arrived, the sun was heating things up, and it was time for my family to plant the garden. My mother wanted to put in yellow beans, which she'd never raised before. She carefully read the planting instructions, her eyeglasses balanced on the end of her nose, "Only plant in full, direct sunlight." She looked up from the seed packet and surveyed the sky and the incoming clouds. It was nearing sunset, and soon it would be dusk. So, my mother put away the packet of seeds for the next day.

My grandmother, by comparison, was a bit more on point when it came to coaxing flowers and vegetables to grow. When I stayed with her in the summers, the first thing she did every morning, after throwing on a robe and taking a cup of coffee in hand, was visit the backyard, enclosed by a tall, red fence, and spend what seemed most of the morning watering, pulling odd, unwanted growths, and harvesting and communing with her lush and thriving garden. It was plain to see that she obtained an immense amount of joy from tending it. And even more joy from cooking and preparing all of her bounty. She also kept large, abundant indoor plants—ferns, palms, a monstrous jade. I once asked her what kind of magic she conjured to keep such flourishing plants. She said, "Not magic, just water." And since she knew that I couldn't keep a cactus alive, she added, "They don't require weaning."

One of my good friends is a gardening scholar. She has written award-winning books, is regularly featured in the *New York Times*, and gives talks and keynotes around the world about gardening, Indigenous food sovereignty, and health. Her most recent book is *Recovering Our Ancestors'*

Gardens: Indigenous Recipes and Guide to Diet and Fitness. She's been at the helm of the Indigenous food sovereignty movement and educates people about precolonial food systems. Like my grandmother, she grows and stores food, year after year, harvested from a well-tended and very robust garden. Despite my having such phenomenal role models, I'm my mother's daughter, "Amelia Bedelia-ing" the seed package instructions and weaning the houseplants. But, conversely, I love gardens. And botany is fascinating. I just don't like the labor necessary to keep a garden. Not to mention the work involved in storing and preserving food.

My partner, Jon, likes growing things, and that's always been a point of endearment to me. He staked out a small section in the back driveway of the property we rent. And saves seeds from the vegetables I buy from the grocery store. But his yields are small because he eschews being orderly or meticulous about planting or tending. This spring he announced that he needed someplace warm and grassy to plant his seed. And then he was struck by lightning.

Lately, Jon's been keen on making salads from dandelion greens he harvests from the yard. My garden scholar friend, who spends hours foraging, advised that dandelion greens are optimal when still shoots, when young. I can't eat them myself. They are beyond bitter. So much for carrying on the hunting and gathering traditions of my ancestors.

I'm in the habit of posting low glycemic dishes on my socials. I joke that I'm writing a decolonial cookbook called "Hoka Hey! Today is a Good Day to Diet!" I'm inspired by all the Facebook photos from different friends harvesting mushrooms, spruce tips, fiddleheads, and wild onions. And lately, I've been seeing articles about eating insects. People eat insects all over the globe, but I don't think I'd like them. I can think of more creative ways to decolonize my diet. For instance, I practice decolonization by stealing from my white neighbors' gardens—taking back the land one ear of corn, and one clump of dirt, at a time. And besides, I imagine if my ancestors were given a choice between nettles, acorns, cattails, or The Cheesecake Factory, they would choose The Cheesecake Factory.

6

Happy Darth Vader Day
Resolving and Letting Go of the Past

A few years ago, an old "boyfriend" from high school reconnected with me on Facebook. I'll call him "Brandon," because everyone was named "Brandon" back in the '80s. "Brandon" was kind of a jerk to me back in high school, so I sent him a photo of a random guy and wrote in my message, "Thanks for reconnecting! A lot has happened since we last saw each other. I'd like you to meet our son, his name is Greg. I guess I probably should have told you that you have a son sooner, but now that I know where you live, you'll be getting served for twenty-eight years of back child support."

Ah, man! That felt good—a relief! Of course, the twenty-eight years of child support was quite exaggerated! But that just made the situation funnier, the idea that he was too freaked out to do the math.

As Father's Day fast approaches, I find myself experiencing waves of that familiar and not uncommon sense of dread and trepidation. What could I possibly have against this day of observance for fatherhood? Hey, it isn't as if I had Darth Vader for a dad—which must have royally sucked for Luke and Leia. No, I struggle with Father's Day because it stirs up old hurts and resentments. Hurts and resentments that might explain why I have held the box of my father's cremains hostage in a storage unit for fourteen years. Or is it sixteen? See? I can't even keep track of the year he died! There's probably some kind of divine law I've been violating all this time by keeping my father's ashes in a permanent time out. I figure it can't be too awful a transgression. He wasn't a spiritual person. And what's a few years in a storage unit compared to eternity? Sometimes I think I should have his cremains made into a garden stepping stone, possibly in the likeness of Darth Vader. And honestly, I would love a garden gnome. My father resembled a gnome, actually, with the beard and round belly, but he was much taller. And not particularly simple nor jolly.

It's nice that so many options are available for cremains memorabilia. A tree urn would be lovely—that's when the cremains are treated so they grow into a tree. A tree! From a red maple to a dogwood to a Japanese flowering cherry. There's a whole menu to choose from, even an indoor plant option. Imagine my father's remains sitting on the credenza in our living room reincarnated as a bonzai tree. That sounds great. Looking over the website, I paused when I got to the Q & A portion, where it explains the following: "In order to turn ashes into a tree, you will first need to be cremated." I assumed I would also need to first be dead. Not that I'm splitting hairs about it.

My high school "boyfriend" "Brandon" might not have known he "fathered" our make-believe son, "Greg," so the fact that he hadn't paid a dime in child support in twenty-eight years isn't his fault. I can be lenient on this point. But my father, the future bonzai tree, the future garden gnome, the future cold storage receptacle? He was not always good to my mom. Or us kids. I don't mean to air my dirty laundry, but he once wrote out a check to my mom that said, "I had to sell a ram for this!" Oh. the audacity! She was so embarrassed taking the check to the bank and seeing the puzzlement cross that teller's face.

That's the thing about dads. Or moms. Or kids, even. We're jerks sometimes. Aren't we? My dad was. Sometimes. We contain multitudes.

Will this be the year I finally make amends, rescue my father's cremains from storage purgatory, and remake him into a plucky, jolly gnome? Maybe.

7

Madam Secretary in the Cabinet

"I promised myself that if Deb Haaland was appointed to serve as Department of the Interior secretary, that I would write an op-ed titled 'Indian in the Cabinet.'"

Jon ignored me and kept looking at the TV.

"Hello? Buh-duh-bum-tsh. Hey, I made a joke, get it?"

"Sure, like a skeleton in the closet," Jon said.

"Huh? No. You haven't heard of *Indian in the Cupboard*?"

"Uh . . ."

"It's a best-selling kid's book that was made into a movie. It's about a miniature eighteenth-century Indian that a little boy finds living in his cupboard."

"Oh? No, I haven't heard of that," Jon said.

So much for my career in comedy. Wah-wah-wah-wah. But seriously, I don't mean to downplay the momentousness of this unprecedented occasion, so I'll clarify what should have been the lede: Deb Haaland, a citizen of the Laguna Pueblo, was confirmed as the first Indigenous U.S. secretary of the interior. And the first Indigenous person to ever serve in a U.S. presidential cabinet.

What does this mean for the United States? It means that the U.S. has a leader who is eminently qualified to protect federal lands and natural resources. Haaland's family tree goes back thirty-five generations on U.S. soil, equivalent to a thousand years, from before America was, well . . . America. And five hundred years before Columbus—you know that dude Natives are always bashing on every year? Who would be better to oversee protection of land and water than an Indigenous person?

Today I stand on my anqcestors' shoulders ready to serve as the first Native American cabinet secretary. Follow me for updates on how we're building back better, protecting our public lands, and creating an equitable clean energy economy for all Americans.

—Secretary Deb Haaland

What does a secretary of the interior do? Madam Secretary Haaland will manage 500 million acres of federal and tribal land. She will oversee relations between the U.S. government and 574 federally recognized Native nations. She will lead the Bureau of Land Management, the United States Geological Survey, the Bureau of Indian Affairs, and the National Park Service. Secretary Haaland will innovate policies for progressive energy that rely less on fossil fuels, like oil and gas, and will move toward clean energy, such as wind and solar.

My life experiences give me hope for the future. If an Indigenous woman from humble beginnings can be confirmed as Secretary of the Interior, our country and its promise still holds true for everyone.

—Secretary Deb Haaland

Why are Indigenous people so thrilled about Secretary Haaland's confirmation? Because for generations Native people have been robbed of our lands, waters, resources, and agency. The "Indian in the cupboard" is actually an apt metaphor for the relationship between the U.S. government and Native peoples, if one considers what little power and visibility Natives have had in determining the management of their own lands and resources. Lands and waters that have been poisoned by uranium, oil pipelines, and nuclear waste. There is immense hope that Secretary Haaland will utilize her position to enact important changes that impact the environment and address climate change.

This is all of our country, this is our mother. You've heard the earth referred to as "Mother Earth." It's difficult to not feel obligated to protect this land, and I feel that every Indigenous person in this country understands that.

—Secretary Deb Haaland

But Tiffany, how do the bears feel about Haaland's appointment? In 2019, while serving as a House representative, Secretary Haaland cosponsored legislation placing federal protections for grizzly bears in the Lower 48. During Haaland's confirmation hearing, her support of the bill was called into question by Senator Steve Daines (R-MT). Haaland answered Daines's question as to why she cosponsored the bill with "I was caring about the bears."

8

Get Out of the Rut and into the Groove

A couple of weeks ago I described to Jon a DIY (Do It Yourself) work-out that consists of bending down and flipping a big tire over. I'd been watching demos on TikTok, a social media platform aptly named for the reminder that one is wasting time—tick-tock, tick-tock—watching repetitive videos on social media. Which implies one's time might be better used by going outside and, oh, I don't know . . . flipping big tires? I mentioned the muscle groups involved in the flipping over of big tires: core, back, glutes. Sounds better than a wheelbarrow of rocks.

I piqued Jon's interest immediately: "I got tires! We can roll them across the street and flip them over in the park!"

It's true. We literally have a pile of snow tires in a corner of our living room; Jon covered them with a sheet, and a handmade sign and his ancestor shrine sit atop the pile, along with a sculpture of his ancestor's head that he made in pottery class.

Despite having such impressive pottery, our living space is not something one might see within the pages of a Pottery Barn catalog—more like *Sanford and Son*. In all earnestness, I would like to roll the tires far, far away, beyond the park, and flip them over forever to the inside of a storage unit.

Flipping over snow tires in the park fits into our lifestyle, which is the opposite of Marie Kondo's streamline, does-it-spark-joy? lifestyle philosophy. Remember her? She is the lifestyle guru who popularized "revolutionary" concepts such as *less is more*. From what I've observed, she had a lot of momentum going until she started telling people they should keep only thirty books; then it was all damage control from there.

What kind of monster would suggest such a thing? I have thirty books shoved inside the oven alone, along with a pile of magazines, not counting the multiple leaning-tower-of-Pisa book collections in every other nook, cranny, and available space inside our apartment.

Jon has another DIY workout routine: he lifts gallon milk jugs filled with water. They work pretty well and are certainly practical, that is until there are literally seven of them spread out on the floor for me to trip over. I don't think Marie Kondo would approve of upcycling. But she might approve of bicep reps, so it evens out.

I'm not actually interested in rolling Jon's snow tires across the street to the park and bending down and flipping them over. Maybe if they were giant tortoises, it would be entertaining. Cow tipping as a sport also seems like it would be fun. But one needs to draw the line, since I doubt very much the animals would appreciate it. I haven't been particularly interested in exercise in the last year—traditional or otherwise. I like to joke and tell people "I feel so great since I stopped working out." However, I wouldn't mind working out with pandas, those super cute, roly-poly ones I see on TikTok videos. And I would probably really enjoy yoga with baby koalas, or baby pigs even. I see ads for yoga combined with a variety of animals and settings. Salsa dancing with velociraptors would interest me. Not actual velociraptors, of course, but dance partners dressed up in those velociraptor costumes.

Whatever kind of exercise I choose, I know I will benefit. It is time to get moving again. But I've been in a winter/COVID-19/social distancing rut. So, I'll need to take baby steps to start, until I get back in the groove.

9

The Native Americans Used
EVERY Part of the Sacred Turkey

Sometimes, I worry that I am overly critical. That I'm using my powers for evil rather than for good. But in my defense, there is so much in the world to criticize. Critical awareness is just the first step toward repairing, restoration, and reconciliation. I strive to balance the criticism with the praise. The celebration with the lament. The complaints with the kudos.

I confess that I've always been highly suspicious of "inspirational culture." I find satire to be a much more fulfilling use of my energy than the world of inspirational messaging. Inspirational memes make me hostile. "Live, Love, Laugh" induces the opposite result of its intention. My preferred message is "Live, Love, Laugh at the Patriarchy."

Believe it or not, there is a whole demographic of people who live on inspirational messages. And I guess that's fine, for them, but I've come to depend on zingers and well-timed barbs. If there were decorative signs of my choosing for sale in home decor departments or Michael's, they would say "I hate myself so good." Or "your beauty is your ugly." Or maybe "babies are annoying." Anti-inspirational messages. I'm the kind of person who would hire Matt Foley, motivational speaker—you know, that big guy who lives in a van down by the river—for my corporate retreat. Because that guy is hilarious.

This is what goes through my mind when I consider the Thanksgiving holiday. Because Thanksgiving represents a fraught and tragic history and is the harbinger of many misunderstandings and ill-founded messages. I have come to consider it the season of "count your blessings" and "being thankful." This seems a safe perspective, where no one can fault me or get offended. Oh sure, even if I don't celebrate Thanksgiving, per se, it never hurts to observe one's gratitude. Even if it seems a little bit cliché. A little bit treacle-y. It's good for the spirit to count one's blessings. Despite . . . well, everything.

There's still cornucopia-plenty to be grateful for.

Yesterday for example, I saw that the Indigenous berry syrup wojapi was featured on Al Roker's new podcast. The Indigenous foods author and chef Sean Sherman swapped out the chokecherries for cranberries, and while that seemed verboten against my grandmas' sauce, it was still pretty amazing to see wojapi receive a national platform.

I am deeply grateful for Indigenous sitcoms, particularly *Rutherford Falls* on NBC's Peacock. And I'm grateful for Hulu's *Reservation Dogs*. And looking forward to more Indigenous-created programs in development. Oh, sure *Longmire* and *Yellowstone* have been cool and everything, but despite those shows casting Indigenous actors, the shows aren't written by or directed by Indigenous creators like *Rutherford Falls* or *Reservation Dogs* are. And it makes a remarkably huge difference.

On that note, I'm grateful for Indigenous humor and comedy. I'm grateful for the people who soldier on, who create content, write, and perform comedy. And for the people who include me in their lists of writers and entertainers of note. This is what rocks my world and brings light to my days.

I'm grateful for all the new books by Indigenous writers, and for there being more opportunities for Indigenous writers than ever before. Some of my favorite books include the anthology of poetry edited by Joy Harjo, our current U.S. poet laureate, *When the Light of the World Was Subdued Our Songs Came Through*. The thriller/mystery novels *The Hatak Witches* by Devon Mihesuah, and Marcie R. Rendon's *Girl Gone Missing*. I'm grateful for so many great books. *Crooked Hallelujah* by Kelli Jo Ford, *The Mason House* by T. Marie Bertineau, *Dog Flowers* by Danielle Geller, and *The Heartbeat of Wounded Knee* by David Treuer. I'm grateful for children's and young adult titles like *Firekeeper's Daughter* by Angeline Boulley, *Apple in the Middle* by Dawn Quigley, and *The Lesser Blessed* by Richard Van Camp.

I'm grateful for the Ojibway word for blueberry pie: miini-baashkiminasigani-biitoosijigani-bakwezhigan. I hope someone publishes a children's book about miini-baashkiminasigani-biitoosijigani-bakwezhigan soon.

I'm grateful for cats, sisters, cheese, and Jason Momoa, not necessarily in that order.

10

Going against the Grain
Isn't Always a Bad Thing

I believe I missed my calling as a shrew. No, not the rodent kind, I mean the "Taming of the Shrew" kind. You know, from the William Shakespeare play? What exactly is a shrew? According to Wikipedia, it is an "unpleasant, ill-tempered woman characterized by scolding, nagging, and aggression." (Don't hold back, tell me how you really feel.)

The term "shrew," or its sister-term, "scold," is considered derogatory and sexist and is usually exclusively applied to women. However, "shrew" was applied to persons of the male persuasion, also—at least at one time, a long time ago. When I think of a modern equivalent for shrews, I think of "Karens." "Karens" have, of course, been around forever, but only very recently have they been added to the lexicon. "Karens" are those dreadful busybodies, usually white women, who get up into other people's business, typically POCs' business—whether that business happens to be bird-watching, enjoying BBQs with friends, or playing fetch with their dogs at the dog park. While Karens are out to ruin everybody's good time, I don't think Karens are an accurate comparison. Because I don't think that shrews are necessarily malevolent.

A shrew can be a Karen, and Karens can be shrews, but that isn't the kind of shrew I aspire to be. Let me just get that straight.

I have an abiding reverence for those members of society often referred to, maybe even unfairly, as "pains-in-the-asses." I think it is possible that clowns, comedians, and jesters are sometimes misinterpreted as shrews. Phyllis Diller and Don Rickles were probably shrews, for instance. Shrews are underestimated and unappreciated in our society, but they serve an important function. Like jesters or clowns, they push back and go against the grain. And, in resisting the status quo, they expose hypocrisy, teach lessons, and bridge conflicts. A shrew might resist for the sheer selfish pleasure of resisting, but what's so terrible about that? Aren't there already too many people pleasers among us? Far too much feigned cheerfulness and toxic positivity? Give me a salty wench or crabby uncle any day of the week. It feels more honest. And let's face it, they're funny. Don't we need antiheroes? Contrary-wises?

My father used to yell at the screen when we were in a crowded movie theater; the movie always had some problem with precision or historical accuracy that he took issue with. Was it embarrassing? Sure. I wanted to hide under my seat and die, but didn't it build character? My grandfather used to blow raspberries if something didn't rise to his high expectations. I don't know if he picked that up from Archie Bunker, his TV fave, or if he'd always blown raspberries. Dad didn't do raspberries, but he flipped the bird a lot. Especially in traffic.

Wikipedia describes shrews as being "stock characters in fiction and folk storytelling." I was fascinated to learn that folklorist Jan Harold Brunvand collected over four hundred written and oral versions of stories containing the shrew leitmotif from thirty different cultural groups in Europe in the middle twentieth century. Who knew that shrew stories were so prevalent? I was even more fascinated to learn that Brunvand created and popularized the theory of urban legends. And that he taught at the University of Idaho in Moscow (where I reside) in the early sixties.

I was surprised to learn being a shrew, or "shrewdom," was a petty criminal offense in the early-modern law of England, during the sixteenth through eighteenth centuries. Petty criminal offense? Would that be a misdemeanor? If you got yourself arrested for being bothersome and contrary in the public square, or belligerent and combative in a crowded auditorium, you'd soon find yourself suffering the consequences with punishments such as a "ducking stool," a "pillory," "jougs," a "shrew's fiddle," or a "scold's bridle." If they sound awful, they are. Some of these punishments, referred to as devices for public humiliation, shaming, and censure, were mentioned in their descriptions as having been used on witches. Yikes, witches!

The bottom line to this, in the final analysis, when it all comes down to it, at the end of the day, when all's said and done, when we get down to brass tacks, when the fat lady sings, when it's all over but the shouting, when the hammer comes down, when all of the i's are dotted and the t's are all crossed, when the cows come home, and my ship finally comes in, the reality is, if you put it like this . . .

It's important to expand our definitions of "shrewdom." And every once in a while give credence to the folks who are annoying.

11

The Goldilocks List

Cold Spots in Moscow

It's super nice that a mortuary in town offered their chapel as a "cooling station" during our heat wave. I imagine they already keep their temps pretty frigid for obvious reasons. I've been meaning to make an appearance so I can "review" it for my venues-to-sit-and-write-at list. Or as I call it, "The Goldilocks List." I call it "The Goldilocks List" because most every place I test sampled last week was unsuitable in one way or another. The venue was either too hard, or too soft, or too noisy, or too hot, etc. . . . but eventually, I did find one that was "just right."

The reason I was playing musical chairs last week is because our tub/shower was being replaced. The work made it necessary for me to vacate the apartment before 8:00 a.m., sometimes 7:00 a.m., and go "hang out" elsewhere. My partner had made plans to be out of town, so the disruption of having no shower, a demolition situation in our home, and figuring out where to spend hours of every day where I might be able to write and get work done, was all on my shoulders.

I hit most of my familiar spots and tried out venues I hadn't visited before. One of my favorite spots is the seating area at Safeway's Starbucks. There's no offending Muzak, the booth seats are comfy, and it's plenty cool. The service clerks are cheerful, even ecstatic, although I'm baffled as to why this is so. I can't imagine that kind of excitement about being on one's feet all day. Don't get me wrong; grocery staff and service workers have been on the front lines taking care of the rest of us for a year and a half, so I don't want to disparage them, I'm grateful! I would just like to know where they're getting their pep, because maybe I want some of what they're having.

While friends had offered to let me hang out at their houses, unlike Goldilocks I was reluctant to intrude. When I posted my situation on Facebook, friends suggested spots I hadn't considered. John's Alley for its Wi-Fi, large tables, and being virtually empty during the day. The Garden, for its good A/C and Wi-Fi. Another friend recommended the pastries at the hospital's cafeteria, and I agree with her there—Gritman's has its attractions, one being LUNCH STAT.

One morning, feeling extra hungry (for porridge, I guess?), I skipped the Breakfast Club and headed to Shari's. I thought I could work there but the elevator Muzak was too distracting—as much as I like Hootie and the Blowfish—the table too low, the chairs too hard. There was an old fella who dumped out bags of change onto his table and spent a half hour sorting them out. It reminded me of the time when I told Jon, my partner, that I had a big bag of change, and he said "well, you better bring it to Washington."

From Shari's I went to One World, and though I was comfortable enough stationed at the big conference table, it was too hot, and the chair cut off the circulation in my legs. I visited Eastside Mall one morning to check out a cute new place serving coffee and pastries. The staff was terrific, and seemed fascinated with my first world problems, and who wouldn't appreciate a sympathetic ear? Even for "issues" as petty as chairs being too hard or a table too noisy. The thing about Eastside Mall, though, is that the playground area, which is undeniably a child's Mecca, second to Willy Wonka's candyland forest, is an echo chamber for the unrelenting joy of children screaming. It's hella loud. And that's fine. For them. It just isn't a place to zone out (or work).

Eventually, I ended up at Dave's Paradise Cafe at the mall. Between the Italian sodas, the cushioned booth seating, and the efficient A/C, I'd hit upon the perfect spot. But it was more than that. They had a good sound system and were playing an '80s mix of songs by Depeche Mode, Echo and the Bunnyman, Tears for Fears, Psychedelic Furs, the Eurythmics, and on and on. I didn't want to leave.

12

My Dakota/Lakota
Grandparents Pray for Ukraine

My Grandma Wing, who said she was related to Sitting Bull, Bear Runs Growling, and Rain in the Face, all renowned Hunkpapa Lakota leaders, was born in 1902, just twelve years after Wounded Knee. The fact that she was born at all during such a tumultuous era, and then lived for ninety-eight years, astounds me. During her long life, she had five children, nine grandchildren, twenty-two great-grandchildren, and sixteen great-great-grandchildren.

I consider myself extremely fortunate to have been present throughout her life, even though she lived in Eastern Montana on the Fort Peck Reservation and my family lived outside Seattle. Every few years, she got on the train with her suitcase packed with gifts and traditional food stuffs, like timpsila (dried prairie turnips) and dried corn and tatanka, and arrived in Seattle to stay with us for a few weeks. And then, of course, every few years my mother would pack up the car during a vacation from work and take us out to Fort Peck to visit her and many of our relatives.

Grandma Wing was mother to Franklin, my sister's dad, who died when she was just a baby. Yet even though I had a different dad, I was still considered her grandchild, and my mother was considered her daughter. Over the years, we came to know our other uncles and aunts, Grandma Wing's other children, and they were always good to us. I loved my Uncle Dale, whom I once visited during a trip to Washington DC, and who drove me around the city and took snapshots of me posing in front of the Washington National Cathedral. Sometime after my parents divorced, he once traveled to Seattle on business, and he and my mother and sister and I all went out to dinner together. He wore a business suit and tie, and I remember imagining that he was my dad. Though I love my white family, and my white dad, it was a novel experience to go out in public like a matching set of luggage—an all-Native family—and imagine that people would assume my uncle was my father.

When my first book was published, he wrote me several pages of his responses and feedback. I had written about his family, after all. His responses were positive, and it was very kind of him to give my book a close reading. He was a deacon at his church and respected in his community. In contrast to Uncle Dale's and Grandma Wing's Christian faith, Aunt Jewel was a pipe carrier. When she visited Seattle with her Meskwaki husband, she gave us all down comforters. I've kept mine all these years later.

I don't know exactly where I am going with these recollections of the Wing side of my family, except to reflect upon how close this branch was to similar circumstances to those unfolding in Ukraine. And this is just one side of our family. There are many other Native relatives from my mother's side: from the Iron Thunders and Brought Plentys of Fort Yates, North Dakota, to others with names like Wise Spirit, Afraid of Eagle, and Two Teeth and Has Horns.

I am a descendant of people who survived invasion and war. The meager allotments passed down to us were once massive tracts of land and territories and resources. And the U.S. government wanted to displace us. And worse. Our lives were expendable and meant very little or nothing.

I know that people are displaced by wars and destruction all the time. And that different countries are full of immigrants and have taken in refugees. It is a deeply troubling reality. But merely acknowledging this doesn't excuse it or bring any comfort.

My Grandma Wing's father, Rev. Basil Reddoor, was a reverend with the Chelsea Presbyterian Church on Fort Peck. He would have been born around 1875, or thereabouts. I have in my possession hymnal books that are written in Dakota. As much as I have mixed feelings about Christianity and church, I recognize that this may have spared my relatives' lives and safeguarded their families.

In the obituary it states that Grandma Wing attended Haskell Institute in Lawrence, Kansas, where she received her high school diploma and a certificate in domestic science. I visited Haskell many times while I was doing a residency at the University of Kansas in 2019. I didn't know until a day ago that Grandma Wing attended there, around 1916 or so. That also astounds me.

If Grandma Wing were still with us, she would be praying for Ukraine. I know she would.

13

Holding Space for Joy in the New Year

Happy New Year, everybody. I hope you had a cozy holiday and got to exchange presents and eat all the figgy pudding and share the specialness of the season. I'm certainly grateful this year that I have someone to watch "It's a Wonderful Life" with and rub my feet—that special someone with whom to share in the existential dread of the daily news cycle.

Nestled in our stockings this year were COVID-19 rapid tests and N95 face masks. "We should tell the kids that test kits are quickies," I said, prepping the swab to pierce Jon's sinus cavity with.

"How heartwarming," Jon said, setting his swab sample in the tester. "This is almost romantic. It reminds me of a pregnancy test. Oh, the nervous anticipation."

"I remember. You kept asking if it was a boy or a girl," I said.

"Congratulations, Ms. Midge, it's COVID!"

It wasn't, of course. We were just joking around, hyper from the candy cane sugar cookies.

Jon was getting ready to have dinner with his family. Everyone was testing beforehand and wearing masks and practicing social distancing. Did they know how to rev up for the Christmas season, or what?

I wasn't feeling up to it because I felt weird about bringing along my portable oxygen and holding conversations with a tube up my nose. I was still recovering from COVID-19 pneumonia. Well, that's not entirely accurate. I always feel weird at large gatherings; they disorient me. One Christmas my mom slipped me one of her pain pills to relax, and I ended up singing German folk songs with my grandmother. In German! I didn't know that I even spoke German, let alone sing folk songs.

I saw articles in *Vogue* and *Glamour* online advertising N-95 face masks—which types are the best, how important upgrading from cloth is, how to prepare for the new variants surging through the population. I feel bad now for wasting my money on fashionable, fun face masks made from cloth. What the hell was I thinking? I bought mermaid cat prints and diva homages, and a Tyrell Corporation owl logo. Maybe when these lethal viruses dial it down to Defcon blue or green we can wear the old masks—the ones that match our outfits. Or something.

It's moot at this point anyway since I have avoided leaving the house. Between The Snowpocalypse and Omicron AND my oxygen tank, the outside place seems triple stacked against me.

Jon teases and says, "What are you saying? You never go outside, anyway."

"Well, sure. But now I don't even have the option. I mean, that's probably worse," I said.

One bright feature of the new year is that I started a new job writing a column for *High Country News* called Heard Around the West. It couldn't be a nicer writing gig. Because while the rest of the daily news teams will be researching and reporting on disasters and climate change, car wrecks and COVID-19 fatalities, I will be combing the internet for stories that make readers laugh. Stories that spark joy. Stories that uplift the human condition. And this really couldn't be a better way to ring in the new year—with a kind of resolution toward holding space for joy. Which will be an intentional practice, a routine.

So let me leave you with this: One story I've been following is about the Grand Teton mama griz and her four cubs—Quad Mom #399. She was tagged at birth, in 1996, and over the years has birthed three sets of triplets in addition to her current quad. She is a mama and grandma to two dozen bears! Photographs of her and her current brood show them foraging on public land throughout Grand Teton Park and Teton National Forest and in the National Elk Refuge. Cams have recorded the family roaming through downtown Jackson Hole. I spent three summers and early falls in Teton Valley, and seeing these bears might have been a religious experience for me, depending on whether I was in a car or exposed in an open field, of course.

I'll keep thinking of those bears, snug and asleep in their den this winter. Just as I am tucked away and snug in my own. I am glad that they don't have the daily news or Twitter updates to bother themselves with. But I also hope they stay out of trouble and get enough to eat.

14

Don't Look Back, Maybe, I Guess?

The New Year's tradition of eating black-eyed peas, greens or cabbage, and cornbread for luck and prosperity seems "normal" enough, depending on one's definition of "normal." But apparently, those black-eyed peas need to be cooked with some "hog jowel" for optimal effectiveness. If you're unsure what "hog jowel" might be, it's exactly as it sounds. Cheek of the pig.

This New Year's Eve I almost committed the grievous error of cooking a pot of chicken soup. Disaster averted. According to the old wives' tales, chickens retrace their scratches, their steps, while it is physically impossible for pigs to look back. Or step back, so it would seem. Clearly, pigs won't be competing on *Dancing with the Stars* anytime soon, unless they're doing all the leading.

Another popular New Year's tradition is the writing of all those end-of-the-year lists, etc. No thanks. Writing "A Year in Review for 2020" seems an emotionally exhausting prospect; major hats off to the brave columnists with the uber-strong stomachs who somehow managed to pull it off. So long 2020 and good riddance. I'm tossing you out like a bad boyfriend. My end-of-the-year review will be in the form of a "Dear John" letter/email/text/Post-it note: "Buh-bye, your s**t's on the lawn. Don't let the screen door smack you on the way out."

In a lot of towns across the U.S. and around the world, people celebrate New Year's Day by jumping into whatever body of water is the coldest. The Polar Bear Plunge. Around these parts the "New Year's baptism" takes place in the Snake River at Hell's Canyon Resort marina. Due to COVID-19, however, the plunge was canceled. Of course, there's nothing stopping anyone from taking a lone dip into the Snake, but be aware there won't be any emergency assistance at the ready. I saw that it was business as usual at Coeur d'Alene's Sanders Beach. The headline read "CdA's Polar Bear Plunge Helps 1,000 People Wash Away Rough 2020." I certainly hope it didn't help a thousand people super-spread COVID-19 to their friends and families. I wonder if the commemorative T-shirt said, "My parents took CdA's Polar Bear Plunge and all I got was this dumb Coronavirus."

As an alternative to end-of-the-year recaps and roundups, I am observing January 1, 2021, as *Don't Look Back, Maybe, I Guess, Day*. My inspiration for *Don't Look Back, Maybe, I Guess, Day* is my friend Sara, who, with her usual aplomb, threw a big party to celebrate her divorce. The last few years with *whatshisface* had been rough, the thorny details of which she had dispatched in our daily morning phone calls. Not wanting to end up a pillar of salt, or worse, Sara made like a pig and refocused her energies. Forward. It worked out well for her.

I'm a citizen of the Hunkpapa Lakota, Standing Rock Sioux Nation. Traditionally, my people (and many other tribal nations) observe the start of the new year in the springtime. The Lakota call it "Wetú, the Moons of Renewal and Growth." Our calendar has thirteen months, or moons, instead of twelve, and our names for the months, or moons, would appeal to poetic sensibilities. Winter is called "Waniyetu, The Cold and Dark Moons." Other names for the winter months are Wanícokan Wi (December), Moon When the Deer Shed their Horns; Wiótehika Wi (January), The Moon When the Sun is Scarce; Cannápopa Wi (February), The Moon of Popping Trees; and Istáwicayazan Wi (March), Moon of Sore Eyes (Snow Blindness). Waniyetu was a special time to hunker down and tell a lot of stories, pass on knowledge. Sort of like Netflix and Chill, but with less screen time, and more IRL F2F.

The song at the end of "It's a Wonderful Life," "Auld Lang Syne," traditionally sung as the clock strikes midnight to observe the passing of the old year into the new, derives from a 1788 Scottish poem by Robert Burns. "Auld Lang Syne" loosely translated means "for the sake of old times." If asked, I can quote only the first line, "should old acquaintance be forgot," before I trail off into *wah-wah-wah* adult-speak from *Peanuts*. It's a bittersweet and touching song in that cliched but sappy way that the expression "in with the old, out with the new" is bittersweet and sappy. I can make exceptions for this year, be as sappy as you want, here at the dawn of 2021, this first month, Wiótehika Wi (January), The Moon When the Sun is Scarce.

15

Is "Native American" Politically Correct?

I had a funny exchange with a health-care worker at the Nimiipuu clinic this week. As she was drawing blood, I asked why the clinic was closed the following day.

She replied, "Mumble mumble."

I didn't make out what she said and asked, "What's that? Say again."

She repeated, "Mumble."

I asked again, "What? Did you say onion?"

She said under her breath, "Indian Days."

"Oh, Indian Days, okay. Hey, wait a sec, did you just whisper 'Indian Days' because you think saying 'Indian' is verboten?"

She said, "Well, yes. I'm from Colorado, I was told I should never say that word."

"Even though you work on the Nez Perce Indian Reservation, for the Indian Health Service?"

One can never be too careful, I guess.

She seemed like a nice young woman, and I did apologize for giving her a rough time.

And it occurred to me that it explains why I so often see "Native American reservation" used in news articles and in the media. That is, on those very rare instances that "Indians," or "Native Americans," make the news cycle. And here I assumed that journalists weren't aware of the actual term. No, I guess they're all from Colorado too.

Last month, a family friend contacted me to ask what the preferred or correct parlance was, currently, for "Native Americans." Her five-year old granddaughter had scolded her for saying "American Indian." And no, she doesn't go to school in Colorado, but in Seattle. I loved that her granddaughter had corrected her so vehemently. I mean, it's adorable. And while I find it amusing, I also recognize the earnest endeavor behind relinquishing what are thought to be disrespectful or antiquated terms. The political incorrectness of it all! One can't say "Indian summer," or "Indian Wars," or "Indian pony?" But instead, one must say "Native American summer," "Native American Wars," or "Native American pony."

I confirmed for my family friend, and her granddaughter, that yes, "Native American" was interchangeable with "Indigenous," that "American Indian" was out of fashion, that many Indigenous people prefer just "Native," because taking on "American" carries certain implications, depending on one's political stance with the colonialist state, and that referring to one's specific tribe is also preferred. My friend understands all that. I'm not sure her granddaughter is able to grasp all the nuances. But she is pretty smart, so you never know. Maybe they'll teach "critical race theory" in the first grade. So far, Kindergarten's done a tip top job.

I figured this was a worthy topic to bring up, because I get asked about it fairly regularly. And I'm always tempted to say, "You can call me 'Native,' or you can call me 'Lakota,' or even 'Indigenous,' just as long as you don't call me late for dinner." That's when you know I've hit my default threshold, when I pull out the Grandpa Jokes.

Sometimes, a well-meaning person will suggest I use the "term" "human." And yes, I agree wholeheartedly on "human" as a signifier, or label. It's downright annoying to separate human beings by these arbitrary identity placemarks, right? Why not just do away with such terms? Political correctness is rubbish. And sure, I'd be right on board with that if it actually meant that persons of color, and Indigenous people, were immediately assessed as "human." But we're not. That's why our universities, our institutions, and our government have human rights task forces and dumb ol' "stuff" like "critical race theory" in place. Maybe when Asian folks aren't being unjustly targeted and violently attacked, or when young Black girls aren't being shot by the police, or when Native

Americans aren't arrested on their own land for protecting their water, then maybe initiatives like "critical race theory" can be withdrawn.

Not to be all pat about it, but I guess it all comes down to affording others common decency. Maybe I shouldn't tease people for their fear of the "I Word." Because, clearly, they're striving to be more compassionate. And that's a good thing. And I don't have anything against Colorado, really. They're human too, after all.

16

Changing Spaces

Assuming all goes according to plan, in the coming days President Biden and Dr. Jill Biden will have installed themselves in the White House, along with their fur children, German shepherds Major and Champ, and a new cat, to be announced! Even though the world's stability hangs in precarious balance, the Bidens will need to get settled in, first things first. I would expect and hope that the gold drapes in the Oval Office are first on their list; they need to be torn down with Berlin Wall furor. Perhaps the dogs' nanny can take a page from the Family von Trapp and repurpose the drapes into sensible rompers for Major and Champ to frisk about in on the White House grounds.

I also fervently hope that the portrait of Andrew Jackson—which former president Trump so carefully culled from the White House's art collection, with which to "grace" his office—will be replaced with something less contemptible and considerably more inspiring. Maybe Tatanka-Iyotanka—Sitting Bull—or Harriet Tubman. But honestly, I'd settle for Daffy Duck at this point.

Making oneself at home in a new space requires considerable finesse. While it wouldn't have been necessary for FLOTUS Jacqueline Kennedy to hire exorcists to extinguish evil spirits after the Eisenhowers moved out, even though Mamie Eisenhower was overly fond of pink, Jacqueline Kennedy assuredly distinguished herself with a historical restoration of the White House. A transformation that not only appealed to her elegant tastes, but was suitable for the life of the White House, and appropriate for the executive quarters representing a nation. Jacqueline brought on a team, one of whom was French designer Stéphane Boudin, whose resume included the restoration of this li'l ol' place called Versailles. Ever hear of it? It's in Europe, or, as I call it, Fancyland.

When my parents bought their first home together, they were as motivated as any incoming presidential couple in remaking their new house into a place all their own. To tailor it according to their own liking, and personal aesthetics. To tear down the ugly drapes and paint over the pink, as it were. To create a showcase worthy of entertaining kings and diplomats, or, in my parents' case, a dining room that pulled double duty: staid family suppers on weekdays and a game/party room for hosting the Andersens and Saturday night poker.

Upon moving in we didn't rent a shaman for any deep spiritual cleansings, as the Bidens undoubtedly should do, but we did rid the house of its decidedly hippie vibe. We replaced all its hippie ephemera—the purple walls, the groovy piles of clutter, the X-rated Popeye and Olive Oyl poster. However, as much as I love my parents and honor their memory, I remain to this day appalled by the decor they chose for our new home, which was as atrocious as it was comical. And sure, I didn't pay rent, so who cares what I thought, but I did have to live there. What was I going to do? Get a job and my own apartment? I was only in the fourth grade. I still believed in Santa Claus.

Their first offense was the new carpeting: an abstract mess of gold and brown flecks, which mightn't have been so bad, really, but wait—it was the exact carpeting used at our local roller-skating rink. Its promise of durability must have sold my father. The carpet was instantly recognized—in that way that *only* roller-skating carpet *can* be recognized—"Hey, isn't this the same carpet as the one at Skate King?!" my friends would ask. And yes, yes it was. Embarrassingly so. There were other faux paus. In lieu of drapes they installed "glass" beads. BEADS. The cat loved them. The lounge units all matched, dark brown thick-cushioned Naugahyde, as if we lived in a gentlemen's club and sat around sipping bourbon and smoking cigars while watching ABC's Afterschool Specials. And in their final desperate cry for help, my parents misappropriated the new kitchen linoleum for the cupboard doors. The linoleum buckled and unstuck in places—a hot mess. I won't go into too much detail because you probably needed to be there to get the full picture.

Moving into a new place presents exciting challenges and hella work. So, join me in offering a big (MAGA) hats off to the Bidens.

17

Heart of the Diamond

Driving past the ball fields near my house the other evening, I experienced waves of nostalgia, the stabby kind, the "aw, gee, shucks" heartwarming kind, worthy of a Hallmark Channel movie. You know for certain spring's arrived when the daffodils push themselves out of the hard, cold earth, and when you see little kids laying siege to the ball fields with mitts bigger than their heads, swinging bats at the plate and running bases with all of their hearts, like it's the last thing they're ever going to do.

I used to be like that.

I was nine years old the spring I pitched for the Eastside Minor League's team the Marigolds. Don't let the name fool you. Marigold might sound like a baby goat from a petting zoo, but we were vicious. We finished first place in the league, having gone head-to-head against the Daffodils, whose pitcher had a mean underhanded fast ball that'd been drilled into her by her relentless father and coach—a guy who, my dad said, had a "bite" like a pit bull.

The Buttercups came in third place, and after them, the Daisies. According to my own relentless coach father, the other teams could have done a lot better, but they were mismanaged and didn't score enough runs because the girls scarfed too much candy during games. Their managers couldn't maintain a simple scorecard, and the batting lineups were a mess because they didn't keep records of the girls' averages.

This was the inaugural year of the newly spawned minor league, the small fries, the pee wee club. Very few of us could throw, catch, or hit a ball to save our lives, but my father worked us over like green army recruits in basic, and we became a ball club worth reckoning with. A team with game. It was only a matter of time until our small fry league got switched out to T-ball, but in my day, in that season, we pitched, and we took balls thrown at our faces, like men. Little men, in pigtails with bits of Bazooka stuck to our faces. My father, our team coach, nicknamed everyone, just like in the big leagues: *Sugarpop, Puckster, Q-tip. Mighty Mouse.* We didn't mess around.

A few years earlier, when we still lived in Snoqualmie Valley, home of dairy cows and Carnation milk, my dad coached a boys' baseball team, the Snoqualmie Bulls. These were large-thumbed and gangling creatures emanating musk and testosterone, hardly boys at all, but olfactory dispensaries who just so happened to walk and talk, catch fly balls, and field base hits. I loved going to games and practices and putting myself to use, fetching bats, balls, and water, all in service of being near them. A batgirl in training.

Naturally, my father wasn't as hard on elementary school girls as he was on his teenage boy players, but somehow he managed to instill in my Marigolds teammates the illusion that we were badass. Our shortstop was extremely small for her age, but she was a coil of muscle with spring action, black grease smeared under her eyes, and a giant ball of gnawed bubble gum in her cheek like it was tobacco. Her nickname was Grand Slam, and she fielded with her older brother's cast-off mitt, three times the size of her hand.

I learned to be a better ballplayer that season, by overcoming my bad habits. My dad took my sister and me to our elementary school field to train. To fix my reflex of being shy of the ball, my dad made me stand behind the chain link backstop while he repeatedly aimed fastballs at my face. And to fix my tendency to step away from the ball when it came my way in the field, he put bats squarely behind my heels, so if I did step back, I'd trip. I learned quickly.

Since my dad coached and my mom managed, I got to pitch, a coveted position in the softball position hierarchy, but one I invariably came by through nepotism.

It was the greatest softball season and the finest and happiest season of my life. I have never felt that valid, that indispensable, since. I occupied center stage, the heart of the diamond, and I felt like a rock star.

18

Poetry Matters

It's better late than never to observe National Poetry Month, which comes around every April first and lasts all month. It was launched in April 1996 by the Academy of American Poets, and, according to Poets.org, "National Poetry Month reminds the public that poets have an integral role to play in our culture and that poetry matters."

What is poetry? And why does it matter? I could ask the same of a lot of things. Why does spirituality or God(dess) matter? Why does professional football matter? As a poet who aspires to be the distinguished poet in residence for Seattle's Space Needle, which isn't an actual appointment yet but very surely should be, I believe poetry is the quotidian made eternal. It is a way to communicate the ordinary and reveal the extraordinary. All this is made possible through poetry, language, and expression.

Whether poetics are considered high art or less than high art; whether about nature or God; about origins, identity, or family. Whether it celebrates or laments; if it centers on the sacred or the profane or somewhere in between; whether it asserts elegy or affirmation; or is concerned with place, regions, lands. While there is certainly poetry extolling the virtues of love and beauty, and one could argue that all poetry is about love and beauty, there is also poetry of avarice and hate, or poetry that catalogs the evils of mankind and even the underworld.

Everyone arrives to poetry differently, and everyone's experience is unique. Some practitioners came to poetry through their love of language, the sound of words, underscored by their understanding of the power of words. Other poets might have felt called to write in order to make sense of the world, to find the words to process their perspective of the world. Or a combination of all these things and more.

Poetry in Song: I came to poetry through community theater. And particularly through musical theater. I sang and chorused and breathed and choreographed and danced through show after show, through song after song, always the chorus and accompaniment. Life is a cabaret, old chum.

Poetry in Flight: I came to poetry through the powwows my mother took us to—city and suburban all-tribes gatherings, dancers replete in their finery and plumage outfitted in feathers of every conceivable color. A cast of hawks, a murder of crows, a siege of herons, a charm of magpies, a host of sparrows, and especially a convocation of eagles. There was always that one little baby making their debut, excited by the drumming; they bounced and darted like a pigeon away from their mother's watchful eye. While the fancydancers flashed and blazed into flames awash in yellows and reds.

Poetry in Motion: I came to poetry through watching my dad play at sporting events at the high school where he taught. There was the infamous game when all the teachers rode on the backs of donkeys up and down the basketball court, giving a new meaning to the term "dribbling." And another memorable game between the teachers and the exhibition basketball team, the Harlem Clowns, which were a Harlem Globetrotters redux.

Poetry in Bloom: I came to poetry through my eighth-grade language arts teacher, who taught *Romeo and Juliet* for the entire quarter. I would not have imagined how equating "love" with "heartbreak" or "passion" with "tragedy" might inform my understanding of "romance" for the rest of my young life.

Poetry in Endowment: I came to poetry through the Celebration Giveaways held on my mom's rez each summer. When Ethel Iron Thunder gifted a Pendleton wrap to Minnie Spotted Elk. When Silas Tail Spins gave 20 pounds of frozen venison to Victoria Walking Child. When John and Myra Two Feathers gave Cain Long Bow $100 toward his college tuition. When Ruby Savior gave Mary and Victor Red Wing a beaded cradleboard for their new baby. When Adam and Vernon Pretty Bird gifted Fortune Buckles a case of chokecherry preserves. Or when Scarlett Comes at Night gifted Ethel Iron Thunder rabbit fur slippers and a matching scarf.

19

Office Supplies Provide Link to the Past

While some lucky couples take romantic trips to Paris or run off to Vegas to get married by Elvis in a heart-shaped chapel, my and Jon's special Valentine's date was uneventful—we drove over to Staples and fondled the office supplies. I bought a power strip with USB plugs, and Jon threatened to buy more printer ink. Of course, the excitement was heightened by the wearing of N95 masks. Fifty Shades of COVID.

Today, it occurred to me that I should title my next book *Office Supplies*, since people seem so genuinely infatuated with them. It's true, isn't it? The fact that there are giant box stores expressly devoted to selling office products is a sure indication that people love them. Crisp new tablets? Check. Mechanical pencils? Check. Post-its? Check. And don't get me started on Sharpies. The fact that some Sharpies contain xylene, a neurotoxin that may damage the organs, holds little deterrent for me. Give me a rainbow-colored pack of Sharpies and I'll follow you to Xanadu, or Office Max, whichever comes first.

My book pitch for *Office Supplies* will present chapters or sections dedicated to the basics, as well as the office favorites: Paperclips. Binder clips. Ode to the Stapler. Hole punchers. Are you salivating yet? Of course, the chapters aren't specifically about office products, per se, but personal and creative explorations of whatever metaphor or theme such and such product might signify.

Take pencils for instance. While being humble and plain objects, there was a time when they dominated the scene. The idea that we all learned to write with one should kind of blow our minds a little. No? I mean, maybe you learned the detailed and complicated art and craft of penmanship by using a crayon or a Sharpie, or maybe you were invited to the chalkboard and practiced your letters with colored chalk, or maybe you had your own old school slate board and slate pencil that cost a whole penny, and you had to sacrifice the horehound candy you planned to buy with the penny you got that year in your Christmas stocking, or buy the stupid slate pencil . . . wait—I digress, that's an episode of *Little House on the Prairie.*

Anyway, maybe you scrawled on rocks or ciphered out your school assignments in dirt—but chances are you used a pencil and paper. Though I don't actually know what children use today. Or whether schools even teach children how to write by hand anymore. I assume they do? Don't they? I mean children aren't taught writing on an Etch-a-Sketch? Or by texting?

My literacy journey consisted of the fan mail I sent to teen celebrities from *Tiger Beat* magazine and the correspondences I maintained with several pen pals around the globe. For several years I exchanged letters with Nigel in Trinidad. He was very sweet. Then I corresponded with a young man who sent me photos of his tongue, yes, his tongue. He seemed terribly insistent that I send him photos of my tongue. His letters were ridiculous and painfully funny to read. Which is why I encouraged him. He typed all his letters on a manual typewriter. I'm certain mine were written on flowery stationery with matching envelopes. I had a lot of fancy stationery. See? It all comes back to office products. I mean, I really love stationery. As a girl, I visited the stationery store near my house frequently, and at one point I convinced my mother to buy me a pen with a giant pink feather at the end—the kind that people buy to sign guestbooks at weddings. The best thing about the stationery store is that I could walk in and buy a single page of decorative paper for twenty cents, if all I had was twenty cents to my name. Or buy a single sticker from the rolls of decorative stickers—a sparkly heart, or a unicorn, or butterflies, or Garfield. I hardly ever used the stickers, they were for collecting. I still collect stickers like a twelve-year-old girl. Except now, since I have slightly more than twenty cents burning a hole in my pocket, I will visit Staples and buy any necessary or trifling thing. But people don't write letters anymore, so there isn't much of a stationery department. And this makes me a little sad. The realization that my visits to Staples, etc. . . . are basically an attempt to time-travel to the old stationery stores I remember.

Earlier this evening, Jon and I watched a scene in *Game of Thrones* where Tywin Lannister wrote a letter with a feathered quill, sprinkled powder on the ink, and then stamped and sealed the letter with melted wax. It was completely and utterly intoxicating.

20

Opening Cans during Perilous Times

Opening cans is the bane of my existence. I'm sorry if my first world problem is offensive, but here's why: the edges of the lids are jagged and scary and seem always to require a second utensil to lift the lid. I mean, no one wants to visit the ER for stitches during a pandemic, right? Whatever's inside the can usually spills out onto the counter, so my hands, of course, get all goopy. Then the lids never actually detach, so with my goopy, wet hands, I twist or jerk the artery-severing disk. The other night, as I performed this perilous ballet, and was whinging on about how impossible opening a can is, Jon said, "Yeah, they should call them cants."

Apparently, can openers are a universal first world problem, maybe even a second world problem, because when I posted about it on Facebook back in June—when we thought the pandemic was over, remember? sigh—and again a couple of weeks ago, I received dozens of responses and comments. Is there a "bad can openers" support group? I don't know, but there seems to be a need for one. The comments I received on Facebook were all extremely helpful, not without comfort and solidarity from same-afflicted comrades. Several friends posted photos of their can openers—KitchenAid, Tupperware, oxo, Black and Decker—and my friend in Seattle posted a photo of his restaurant grade device, which had been retrofitted into his studio apartment kitchenette countertop. Impressive.

While a discussion about can openers might seem banal, decidedly unsexy—are you still awake?—it's clearly a topic that people are passionate about.

The biggest complaint in the discussion thread was that can openers needed to be replaced every year, or every few months. Really? If most of the first world, or second world, is throwing away their old ones and buying new ones every year, that's a lot of can openers. Is this a conspiracy? Or planned obsolescence? And I'll bet no one is throwing out the old ones. I bet they just get stashed in a cabinet or drawer, entombed, somewhere in the house, like King Tutankhamun—no one knows why. It's complicated and seems illegal, somehow. We're talking about hardware, a tool. One doesn't simply throw those away. Do they?

Some of my Facebook friends suggested surefire solutions, devices they swore by, such as a U.S. Marine can opener from the '60s, attached to a keychain. An added bonus: the sharp hook on a hinge that loosens and tightens screws. Another friend suggested sharpening those useless blades by using a fine, flat file and turning the handle to rotate the blade. My friend in Nebraska said to look in thrift stores for "old case-hardened steel ones," though I am not sure what "old case-hardened" means.

There is a cartoon that makes the rounds now and again—it might be a Far Side cartoon—that depicts a couple in a basement bomb shelter. In the moment that mushroom clouds are exploding in the world above them, the wife is saying to the husband, "How many times did I say it, Harold? How many times? 'Make sure that bomb shelter's got a can opener—ain't much good without a can opener,' I said."

There might even be a *Twilight Zone* episode with the same dilemma. However, maybe it isn't quite as dire as first imagined, because there are a few life hacks for opening a can without using a can opener. You can Google it. I wouldn't want to use them unless it was an emergency, because they seem messy and potentially hazardous, but with the way the world is going right now, who knows? Maybe it wouldn't be such a bad idea to refine this skill. You never know when you might need to open up a can of whoop-ass.

21

Open Mouth, Insert Foot; the Man is a Human Train Wreck

"We birthed a nation from nothing. I mean, there was nothing here. I mean, yes we have Native Americans but candidly there isn't much Native American culture in American culture."—Rick Santorum's address at the Young America's Foundation summit.

One week the media reports that Indigenous people are "nothing," and the next week we're flagrantly dismissed as "something else." Which is it? "Nothing?" Or "something else?" Make up your minds. We're accustomed to our sociodemographic being minimized as "other"; it's old hat, this uninspired erasure.

"Something else" refers to the CNN election coverage back in November, when a poll broke down voters by ethnicity; per usual Native Americans weren't included among the Latinx, Black, or Asian population, but instead of the customary "other," Native Americans were lumped in with "something else."

Sure, this isn't the first time Rick Santorum has sh** the bed, and I'm sure it won't be his last. He's famous for his outrageously offensive statements. He's a human version of a train wreck. This is a man who opined opposition to gay marriage by saying marriage isn't "man on child, man on dog, or whatever the case may be." Really, Rick? You're sure about that?

Santorum's statement about "birthing a nation" hits a little too close to the bone. Ever hear of a film called *The Birth of a Nation*? It is considered to be the most controversial and racist U.S. film ever made. The film made heroes out of the KKK, while portraying African Americans—played mostly by white actors in blackface—in the worst possible ways. So, when Santorum makes speeches that include veiled references to the most incendiary film of its day, it suggests that he is signaling to white supremacist factions. Duh.

Several Native journalists have pointed out that Santorum's comments indicate how poor a job the U.S. has done in including accurate school curricula with regards to our nation's relationship with Native Americans. That is an understatement and, of course, it's true. However, I'm not going to give Santorum a pass that easily. His comments are not mere ignorance, or a lack of historical literacy. They represent his anti-Indigenous views and moreover, I believe, were intended as such.

It's beyond an affront to state that nothing existed on the continent at the time of first contact, and in the decades and centuries following. And to espouse such a thoroughly reprehensible idea is to deny cultural genocide of Indigenous people. Holocaust deniers aren't exclusive to the European and Jewish Holocaust. There are currently 574 federally recognized tribes in the United States. And that number was far higher at first contact, when the Indigenous population of the Americas is estimated to have been as high as 118 million. The influence and contributions of Indigenous cultures to the world are limitless.

The very foundation of the United States is tied in with the original peoples. Democracy, the formation of the United States of America, and the U.S. Constitution were inspired by the ancient Iroquois "Great League of Peace." The Iroquois Confederacy is the oldest living democracy on earth and was acknowledged as such in 1988 by the U.S. Senate: "The confederation of the original thirteen colonies into one republic was influenced by the political system developed by the Iroquois Confederacy, as were many of the democratic principles which were incorporated into the constitution itself."

To state that there isn't much Native American culture in American culture is like stating the earth is flat, or bears don't go to the bathroom in the woods. Indigenous contributions are seen the world over. In agriculture, food systems, architecture, military, arts, music, literature and entertainment, sports, science, and space exploration, not to mention millions of tracts of land, waterways, and natural resources.

The National Congress of American Indians (NCAI), the Native American Journalist Association, and many other organizations and Indigenous thought leaders have urged CNN to dismiss Santorum from his position as a senior political commentator. As of this writing, CNN has yet to make a statement.

22

Scene from a Clinic's Waiting Room
A Cautionary Tale

Whenever I visit the tribal clinic around this time of year, I'm reminded of the young guy I saw a few years ago, on the Lummi rez, who had injured his hand in a fireworks accident. While his injury had been severe, the first thing I noticed about him was that he was carrying around a weird stuffed doll like a purse. The doll was two-headed, part cat and part Raggedy-Ann, dressed in black and white striped stockings with large black buttons for eyes. It was the sort of doll that I imagined Marilyn Manson might have had as a child.

The injured guy looked around fourteen. His hand was amply covered with gauze, and his elbow was propped up with a stick, in a perpetual wave. His manner was strange, but then I realized he was under the influence of pain medication. His mother was sorting out all of his medical information with the nurse, while the boy sat in the lounge waiting on prescriptions, regaling everyone else in the waiting room with the details of his injury.

A younger boy seemed in total admiration of him, his little face looking up at him, just beaming. "It was rad!" the gauzed boy said. "Blood was spurting out like a fountain, all over the place. I've never seen blood projectile like that, except in the movies."

The younger boy asked, "What fingers again?"

An older couple was sitting and listening.

The older boy said, "The tips of these three fingers are gone, they had to amputate this one, it was so shredded. The skin from all the way down to my wrist is totally gone. There's nothing left but bone. Weird it didn't even hurt, I was in shock, you know? Even when I was getting fixed at the hospital, I was all, joking and stuff. I was all like 'dude, can I keep that finger bone?' I want to make a necklace out of it."

The younger boy's mother nudged her son. "Are you paying close attention? This is what can happen if you mess with pipe bombs and fireworks. Don't you ever do that!"

The gauzed boy's mother was asking people about getting information out to kids about firework safety. "Look at what happens!" she said. "That'll get the message across faster than anything else! It's weird because reservations have no limitations about the sale of explosives— that's what a lot of these fireworks are, explosives!"

The gauzed boy was a school athlete, with the body of a dancer. His long, black hair fell into his eyes. I had heard his mother telling another woman in the main waiting area that he ran track and read novels voraciously; she said that her son read so much everyone gave him flack for being "so weird."

I sat eavesdropping on the conversation. He was excited about getting a steel prosthetic for his fingers——just like the guitarist from Black Sabbath, who apparently had his fingers amputated just for the privilege of looking like a Borg.

The elderly woman asked the younger boy's mother, a really pretty woman who worked for public service and wrote grants, if she was married and did she know her son?

"Arthur?" the younger boy's mother asked. "Oh, yes, I know Arthur. But I have a boyfriend."

The gauzed boy's mother complained to the admin clerk in reception.

"Harborview assured me that it was all going to be taken care of by Lummi. Now they're not? Somebody's going to do something about this."

The younger boy's mother leaned over to the elderly couple, "Her husband is on the tribal board." The elderly couple nodded knowingly.

The gauzed boy and his mother gathered their things, said their good-byes to the people in the waiting area, and exited down the hall. The gauzed boy seemed to be swooning, carrying his two-headed Marilyn Mansonesque doll, while his mom clucked and bickered at him like a crow. The younger boy whispered to his mother, "She was really mad."

23

Some Pig in a *Brave New World*

Just when I think I'm having a bad day—like when I am making the bed and I find a banana peel among the sheets and I suddenly realize that I slept with said banana peel under the covers all night like an orangutan—well, nothing can compete with those crushing moments as much as reading a news story about a successful pig-to-human heart transplant. And here I thought I had it so bad. What's a little compost in my bed compared to having a pig's heart?

Recently, surgeons at the University of Maryland School of Medicine successfully transplanted a pig's heart into David Bennett, a fifty-seven-year-old man suffering from heart disease and arrhythmia. The pig had been genetically modified so that its genes would be compatible with human ones. This science brings up a lot of questions regarding animal welfare. While it's true we raise pigs—and lots of other animals—expressly for the purpose of slaughter and consumption, what are the ethical implications of conducting medical research on a pig? In particular, raising pigs in a lab and tinkering with their DNA before harvesting their organs. That's a very big question, and I don't have any quick answers.

The researchers who successfully transplanted the pig's heart into the patient have been working on animal-to-human organ transplants for the last thirty years, and the research has gone on even longer. In 2016, pig hearts survived, and kept beating away, inside the abdominal cavities of baboons for over two years. It sounds like a horror movie, but it's true.

Last September, a surgical team at the University of Alabama at Birmingham successfully implanted the kidneys of a genetically altered pig into James Parsons, a fifty-seven-year-old carpenter from Huntsville, Alabama, who days earlier had been rendered brain-dead after a dirt bike accident. The pig kidneys functioned without any sign of rejection for over three days, before Parsons was removed from life support.

The idea of animal-to-human organ transplants, or xenotransplantation, might sound repugnant, but the demand for organs is critical. Last year there were 41,000 transplants performed in the U.S. with over 100,000 people that still remain on the national waiting list.

The fact is humans have been "tinkering with" and harvesting from our animal brethren since forever. We justify our use of animals, from shoe leather to wool to goose down, despite the fact that many of these industries are quite brutal. Xenotransplantation just ushers in another iteration of animal extraction. And while using an entire pig heart for transplants is brand new, using parts of pig, bovine, and horse heart valves is not. These heart-to-heart transplants have been happening for years—for over thirty years, actually.

While humans are cruel to animals in a myriad of ways, aren't humans also cruel to other humans? Why yes, we are. Understatement. Not that our cruelty to each other justifies our cruelty to animals, but, at least for the time being, I haven't seen any Soylent Green situations on the news. And while people reuse body parts from other humans who've died, as far as I know there is no evil overlord corporation that farms humans for the purpose of harvesting their organs. A close call might be the use of infant boys' foreskins to make beauty creams and stem cells, which is very *Brave New World*. And blood donation, which is understandably necessary and good, may be as necessary and good as harvesting the cerulean blood from horseshoe crabs as well as kidney donation—thank you to the brave and altruistic souls who undergo that trial. And to those people in third world circumstances who are "forced" to sell a kidney due to extreme poverty and hardship—which is really just another kind of factory farm, isn't it?

What do clergy think of pig heart transplants—whole hog, not just the valve? That would depend on who is being asked. Dr. R. Albert Mohler, president of The Southern Baptist Theological Seminary, has concerns about animal-to-human transplants: "We're talking about something that is truly ominous even if truly promising. The ominous part comes from the fact that when you're talking about different species, you are talking about different genomes, different genetic structures." Despite Dr. Mohler's concerns, he is in favor of the procedure. Physician and theologian Andrea Vicini, S. J., of Boston College stated: "It seems to me [the medical team was] very careful in addressing the major [ethical] concerns from a medical point of view . . . informing the patient and not making false promises about . . . the expected outcome."

Given the choice, surviving with a transplanted pig's heart or chronic heart disease and death, which would you choose?

24

Waist-Deep in Crocodiles
We Can't Afford to Be Cavalier about Mask Mandates

I watched the news reports in horror as Texans froze inside their homes, with no lights or electricity and no running water due to frozen pipes. And it seemed clear from the news reports that some Texas and government officials didn't care all that much about the magnitude of human suffering, or the deaths and destruction that resulted.

I watched in horror as a friend updated her perilous situation on social media. Both she and her husband had COVID, in a freezing house, with no water or power. Fortunately, friends helped with water, a generator, and medicine. They're both okay and out of the woods, but what a frightening ordeal. How vulnerable we are to the whims and missteps of a select few in control of our lives.

Right on the heels of the humanitarian crisis in Texas, today I saw the announcement that Governor Greg Abbott is reopening the state. He tweeted "I just announced Texas is OPEN 100%. EVERYTHING"—like he was selling appliances for an end-of-the-year clearance sale. And as if an afterthought, a proverbial cherry on top of his sundae, he added, "I also ended the statewide mask mandate." I kept waiting for the "wink wink" emoji. Or a "Haha!" Before realizing he was 100 percent all caps serious. It wasn't ALL ITEMS MUST GO, but ALL PEOPLE MUST GO, apparently. Which is likely the memo Senator Ted Cruz received, except he read it as "all people must go to Cancún for pina coladas."

I'm probably just overreacting. What is there to raise alarm about, anyway? Currently, 3,000 Americans are dying from COVID every day.

But, by all means, open states up and eliminate mask mandates. And just for fun why not liberate all the tigers from the zoos. Let loose the grizzly bears. Release the Kraken. Shouldn't we all make a run to Cancún for pina coladas? And while we're there, let's drink the water. I double dare you. We're already waist-deep in crocodiles, what difference would it make?

Isn't this cavalier attitude about masks and social distancing part of the reason why over 500,000 people have died? Last week I worked myself up into a lather because our apartment manager informed us that workers would be installing a nonessential, nonemergency item in our bathroom. The next day. This immediately raised alarm. I imagined streams of unmasked workers stomping through our living space, spreading dangerous pathogens in their wake. There was zero mention of taking precautions and no acknowledgment of our concerns. A friend of mine contracted COVID from workers coming into her rental. She sat up nights breathing with an oxygen tank. Fortunately, we were able to fend them off. And I probably shouldn't have kicked up such a fuss. But I kept imagining a herd of rhinos crashing through the walls of our apartment. I kept imagining a wild Jumanji situation.

I'm due for my second helping of the Moderna vaccine on the eighteenth. I receive health care through the Indian Health Service and was able to get vaccinated at the Nimiipuu tribal casino. My sister was vaccinated at the Seattle Indian Health Board, even though she has excellent insurance and health care through her job. The mortality rates among Indigenous people are twice that of white people. *The Guardian* reported, "Nationwide one in every 475 Native Americans has died from COVID since the start of the pandemic, compared with one in every 825 white Americans and one in every 645 Black Americans."

I keep thinking if only science deniers like Governor Abbott were half as incensed about the number of Americans dying from COVID as they are about the discontinuation of a handful of racist Dr. Seuss books, we'd be in much better shape. If only there were half as much outrage pointed at the fatalities in Texas due to its power outages as there is about Mr. Potato Head, we might have a chance.

25

The Holiday Dinner Basket

It was a two-story house, unpainted and weather-beaten, the roof covered with yellow moss. The yard had amassed overgrown bushes and weeds; thorny trellises and ivy ascended from the foundation. There was no path to the door, just caked earth, more weeds, and a couple of rickety steps that my grandmother illuminated with a small flashlight. A firm knock, once, twice, three times. "Mr. Know? It's Gertrude Midge." No response from inside.

The interior was lit by small candles, visible through the gauze curtain in the upper window. Some years there was evidence of a woodstove as gray smoke crept out of the chimney into the night's sky. Tap, tap, tap. "Mr. Know? Merry Christmas! I've brought you a dinner basket," my grandmother called out.

Everything about the house seemed to defy gravity. It appeared to lift itself from its foundation, from the very earth, and tip itself heavenward. It thirsted, that house. I can't think of any other way to describe it. When its occupant is invisible, the house itself takes on their form. But beyond a mere mortal form. It becomes imaginary, magic from a child's waking dream.

At Thanksgiving and Christmas every year, my grandmother bundled up our dinner leftovers, replete with an extra helping of pie—pumpkin or mincemeat—and we walked the few short blocks down Chestnut Street—past all the other houses full of families, much like ours, enjoying their dinners and celebrating the holiday— to Mr. Know's dilapidated house on the corner lot. The contrast between Mr. Know's house and all the other houses on the street was startling. On December 25th the other houses vibrated with life, Christmas lights blinking and bright, illuminated with Yuletide spirit. And then there was this dark, empty-looking dwelling. A haunting on that corner lot amid all the treacle, all the glow.

The porch was a dark mouth in which we offered the holiday food. In all those years Mr. Know never once came to the door. My grandmother would call out to the man, the specter, behind the shutters, "Mr. Know, it's Gertrude Midge, I've left you a basket." My grandmother, infinitely optimistic, always waited, expectant each time that this was the year he might emerge. But he never did.

Some years I entertained the possibility that Mr. Know didn't exist, that my grandmother had perhaps invented him in order to demonstrate acts of charity to those less fortunate. Other years, I was convinced that Mr. Know was an all-knowing, all-wise oracle, and our annual offerings were payments for the auspicious fortunes he granted, like tithing, or offering a sacrifice. Had I been intended as a sacrifice? Surely not, what a preposterous idea! Save it for one of my stories! I told myself.

I never once met or glimpsed Mr. Know. Even when I visited my grandparents outside of the holidays. I would be riding my bike or walking through the neighborhood and suddenly realize that I was passing by Mr. Know's house, but in the brightness of day. I'd circle back or slow down so I could study the house and property, scanning for any sign of life inside. Searching for Mr. Know. Of course, I never saw him. But in later years, my grandmother would remark that she'd seen him. She relayed that he'd been getting out from under his hermitage, that she saw him at the senior center or browsing the aisles at the market. "It's so good to see him out and about after so many years shut in." But she never knew the cause of this change in him. I don't have any memory of delivering holiday meals to him beyond my childhood. By the time Mr. Know joined society, I must have been grown.

It seems just a few years ago, but it is really more like two decades ago or longer, after my grandparents had passed, that my aunt discovered Mr. Know had died and donated his life savings—more than three hundred thousand dollars—to the youth services organization in Auburn, Washington.

26

Things That Don't Make Sense but Should

The other day I saw a commercial with a bunch of people working in a dog treat factory. Every worker was wearing a hair net or head covering. I thought, why? Have they never noticed what dogs will typically eat on any given day? I will spare you the details, because if you've ever had a dog then you already know. But seriously, a few stray hairs are the last thing anyone should worry about.

My little Pomeranian, Gus, once hauled off with a set of dentures belonging to our host. Fortunately, they were found later on the front lawn and in reasonably good shape. Gus also took off with the same host's hearing aid. These are not items that one can afford to lose to a fifteen-pound dog who thinks they are his personal chew toys.

Another thing that doesn't make sense is the fact that universities don't have valet parking. Some say parking on college campuses is a nightmare, which, depending on one's situation, it could very well be. Just because something is a first world problem doesn't mean it's exempt from being a horrible inconvenience that could use some improvement. My partner, Jon, suggested an app for a valet parking system, to avoid having to walk uphill in the rain, sleet, or snow in both directions. Jon also suggested a system of rickshaws—consider it conditioning training for college athletes. Another underutilized source of manpower, the way I see it.

Another thing that doesn't make sense is the fact that I never get tired of patting myself on the back. Especially when it comes to outsmarting my genius partner. One afternoon this last winter, I walked into the kitchen and smelled something burning—like electrical burning. I called to Jon in the other room to come to the kitchen and help me detect its source. We both sniffed everything in the kitchen—the stove, the light fixtures, behind the fridge, all the usual suspects. We sniffed and sniffed like a couple of bloodhounds, but nothing, no source. We gave up and said we'd wait and see. Jon went back to his desk, which isn't actually a desk but a partially caved-in card table I found at the thrift store, with a desktop computer atop it and a bouncy ball for a chair, I call the Sittin' Ball. I lingered a few moments, sniffing, sniffing, until it occurred to me to check the heating elements in the dining area. Good call. The smell was coming from Jon's wet shoes leaned up against the heating vent. This pleased me to no end, to have outsmarted a trained electrical engineer.

Of course, this reminded me of the time I fixed the washing machine, following Jon's painstaking troubleshooting sessions. And the time I fixed his laptop. Both times I had suggested unplugging and plugging it back in, as with the washing machine, and shutting down and removing the battery before restarting, and both times this worked like a charm.

One time I couldn't access a certain clearance system for the software I was using for a college writing contest. And after troubleshooting with an expert IT guy for most of an hour, it occurred to me to suggest reconciling the passcode with the one I had been given. And yep, that was the trouble: the passcode had been off by one lowercase letter. It surprises me that the easiest solutions aren't the first things professionals try. Makes no sense, right? These solutions coming from someone who smudges with sage whenever I need to use the printer.

It's like when Jon loses something—his wallet, his glasses, or his keys. I always seem to know exactly where his misplaced items are. As if my uterus is some kind of homing device. It's a superpower. One morning Jon woke me up out of a dead sleep because he couldn't find his keys.

I said, "Look in your pants pockets."

He said, "I did look and they aren't there."

I said, "No, look in the other pocket."

He said, "I looked and I'm late, and . . . oh. I didn't look in that pocket. Never mind."

27

Agape, Actually

Celebrating Valentine's Day in Quarantine

With Valentine's Day just around the corner, it's never too soon to start thinking about what sorts of gifts to bestow upon your "beloved." "Beloved" is a loose term. Too often Valentine's Day is associated with and exclusively targeted toward what the Greeks termed "eros"—the passionate, physical love between consenting, hetero, cis, white, conventionally attractive Christian adults between the ages of nineteen and thirty-two with a penchant for refurbished midcentury furniture and locally sourced natural fabrics. A target demographic commonly featured in Lifetime movies and *Love, Actually*.

But I prefer to consider all the other permutations of love. Such as "agape," which describes one's love for their fellow human, or God. Unfortunately, we tend to forget our sense of "agape," especially during rush hour traffic and presidential elections. So, it is important to extend charity and compassion to your fellow travelers. For example, yesterday at Safeway I offered to let an old guy with a jug of milk go ahead of me in line. It's important to make sacrifices for the common good.

And besides, "eros" type love and desire is exhausting. Even the Greeks were suspicious of erotic love. They felt it brought confusion and irrepressible feelings—that it "loosened the limbs and weakened the mind." Not exactly a ringing endorsement. Personally, I don't have this issue, because I've been with my partner for a decade. We're best described as an old married couple, as in, "You're so good together, so in sync, you finish each other's sandwiches." Yep, Fifty Shades of Grey Poupon; that's when your relationship has officially entered the platonic zone, the stage when the prospect of sandwiches becomes more exciting than sex.

Still, what's the harm in celebrating Valentine's Day? I mean, there's chocolates, right? It's just as important to demonstrate love for your sweetheart, your children, and even your coworkers, as it is to demonstrate love for the guy standing behind you holding a jug of milk at Safeway. Go ahead. Be random and terrifying. Tell the mail carrier you love them. Throw Hershey's Kisses out the car window at pedestrians. Make your partner a sandwich for no reason, and then finish it for them.

When it comes to Valentine's Day gift-giving, remember to keep it creative. Any knucklehead with two nickels to rub together can buy a heart-shaped box of candy. And no one is going to hold a grudge against you if they aren't presented with a diamond tennis bracelet or an emerald tiara. It's irresistible to gift your lover with a twenty-five-cent plastic ring procured from the gumball machine at the local grocery store. Who said romance has to be expensive?

Many, many years ago, sometime just after the Ice Age, my paramour gave me a big, juicy beef heart. And then prepared it for our Valentine's dinner. Pretty gol-darned romantic, no? Never underestimate the enchanting effect of organ meat. It's better to stay home and cook, anyway. I mean these days, especially because of the pandemic. No one's going to want COVID-19 for Valentine's, I assure you.

Here are some surefire Valentine's Day gifts that say "gosh, you're neat."

Individually wrap bananas in aluminum foil and arrange them in a used Amazon mailer. They're almost as nice as a specialty crate of pears from Harry and David's.

A coupon to redeem for a romantic game of chess while role-playing characters from "The Queen's Gambit." Hubba, hubba, checkmate.

A hand-knitted scarf made from yarn spun from your quarantine hair.

If you've been quarantined with your partner the last eleven months, they're probably sick of you. Give them the premium Valentine's gift of 24–48 hours of solitude.

A Netflix subscription. Ha! Just kidding. Of course, you already have one.

Hickory Farms is selling "love bites." Because nothing says "soulmates forever" like a hunk of salami and a handful of cheddar wedges.

A new pair of quarantine sweatpants.

Stock purchases in whatever the next GameStop ploy will be.

A romantic votive candle which, when lighted, discreetly signals your partner to make you a PB&J sandwich.

28

I Had COVID-19 and
Spent the Week in the Hospital

Last week the father of one of my closest friends died from COVID. I didn't hear the devastating news for more than a week, however, because I was receiving care for COVID pneumonia in the hospital and she felt it best not to tell me. So, yeah, that happened. Although I've been reading all the stories and reports and monitoring the statistics on all the people who have lost their lives to COVID these last two years, my friend's dad is the closest connection I've had to one of COVID's victims. And, of course, my friend and her family are also victims. All of the families and friends, coworkers, and communities of those who have died from COVID are victims. And it hasn't stopped. The reports say that the new variants will continue to surge and continue to make even more people sick, and then even more people will lose their lives and be mourned by their families, friends, coworkers, and communities.

The world is terrifying.

Even though I was vaccinated (but hadn't yet gotten a booster), I still contracted breakthrough COVID. My partner also came down with COVID. But because I have certain health setbacks, I ended up in the hospital, while he came out relatively unscathed (crossing fingers). Being hospitalized is not an experience I ever want to repeat, if I can help it, but I am grateful that I received several IV drip doses of Remdesivir, and that I received oxygen, and that I was monitored and cared for. I spent four nights in the hospital, four sleepless, crappy, lonely, uncomfortable nights. On my stomach. In the recommended "planing" position. Upon first being received into my room, I was welcomed by way of the respiratory therapist on duty reading me the riot act, lest I not comply with regulations. I felt like I had stepped into the scene from the film *Full Metal Jacket* with the drill sergeant yelling into my face threatening to "screw off my head and sh** down my neck." At one point they took a break from hollering at me and softened their tone by explaining "I can be a bitch, but it's only because I care." Ah, a method to their madness! I'd have to say their methods worked, because whenever I felt even the slightest bit compelled to turn onto my side, I saw the therapist's looming face in my mind's eye and remained on my belly, fearful that they might call their guy Vito to bust my thumbs and steal my wallet. This intimidation was in the interest of healing me. And keeping me off a ventilator. When asked if I would submit to a ventilator, I said no. I had no interest in being vented. When, actually, I didn't anticipate that it would ever come to that. But what do I know?

I was the only patient in the COVID section for most of my time there. And I must have met and been poked, punched holes into, prodded, bled, cuffed, and shot by fifty or more health-care personnel. It was hard to keep anyone straight because everyone was masked, gowned, and wearing a helmet or welding headgear. It took two days of requesting Tylenol before anyone finally brought me a dose. At one point a patient advocate came to my room to talk to me because I had made a fuss about my IV injection spot becoming inflamed and excruciating. I had been refusing a new IV because it felt traumatic and I wanted a break. The nurse who pulled it out of my arm took little care at all and literally ripped out my hair beneath the starburst of awful tape. I screamed. And I hollered. Why? It hurt like hell. A care worker told me that often patients get paranoid and start believing in conspiracy theories. As if that were an explanation for me. At 3:00 a.m. a different nurse snuck into my room while I was half-asleep and punched a hole in the back of my dominant hand for the new IV. I asked her to put it in the other hand, and she scoffed at me. I asked her for a Tylenol, and she argued with me, asking me whatever did I think I needed Tylenol for? I literally couldn't move my hand. I called the nurse station and asked to change the IV and was told I'd have to wait. It was a drama.

I'm especially grateful to the care workers who took good care of me. All 976 of them, coming and going, and bringing me ice and Band-Aids and applesauce and resetting my alarms, bells, and whistles and putting stethoscopes to my lungs to listen for that nasty "crackle."

I'm home now, tethered by a blue tube to a big gray lung heaving in the corner of the living room. My blood oxygen levels are still on the low side, so I don't know how much longer I have to worry about them. I've been sleeping, decadently, on my side, not in "plane position," and I hope it doesn't off me. I do feel stronger, though. And that is reassuring. Except for the fear of ever leaving the house, or my partner leaving the house, and getting COVID again, everything's great. I'm grateful for all the well wishes, the check-ins, the lovely gifts, and for family and friends bringing meals and groceries. I hope more people who are able to get vaccinated will get vaccinated, and I hope that everyone, and I mean everyone, will *please* mask the F up.

2 *High Country News, Heard Around the West*

Mishaps and Mayhem
from around the Region

29

Free Bird, Lost-and-Found Bear, and Cowboy Pride, February 2022

Oregon

A rather sociable resident of Grants Pass sought out the company of delighted schoolkids at Allen Dale Elementary School in November. *The Oregonian* reported that the special guest peeked into classrooms and pecked politely on doors before making his way inside to help himself to snacks, even perching atop some students' heads for a chat. The visitor, as you may have guessed, was not a human, but a talking crow, or maybe raven, named Cosmo. Cosmo regaled both students and teachers with remarks like "What's up?" and "I'm fine." Cosmo also demonstrated a full command of expletives, though *The Oregonian* did not disclose exactly which ones. Animal control officers were called to the scene, but they determined that capturing the controversial corvid was out of their jurisdiction. A wildlife officer from Oregon State Police also failed to net Cosmo, who made a game out of the capture attempts while the entire student body cheered it on. After the cops gave up, Cosmo retired in triumph and ended up spending the night outside the school. Eventually, his caretaker, Daphnie Colpron, who had been distraught over the bird's disappearance during Thanksgiving weekend, was alerted. Cosmo was returned to her home, though Colpron insists that he remains a free bird. We think he has a good career ahead as a substitute teacher and are looking forward to his classroom remarks on the work of Edgar Allen Poe.

Montana

This is not your typical Montana story about a bear, though it is sure to knock the stuffing out of even the most stoic among us. In 2020 six-year-old Naomi Pascal and her family were hiking in Glacier National Park when she lost her teddy bear along one of the trails, KPAX reported. What made this teddy bear particularly special is that it had been with Naomi since she was adopted from an Ethiopian orphanage—it was an introductory gift from her new parents, Ben and Addie Pascal. Naomi and Teddy have had many adventures together, visiting Ethiopia, Rwanda, Greece, and Croatia with their new family. But when the bear was lost, Naomi and her family assumed they would never see it again. Fate intervened when an intuitive park ranger and bear specialist, Tom Mazzarisi, found the teddy bear in a pile of snow and rescued it. Usually such items are tossed, Mazzarisi said, but in this case he relented and allowed the teddy bear to ride along with him on the dash of his patrol truck. What followed is a whole lot of kismet.

A Michigan woman visiting Glacier the following September spotted the teddy on the dash of Mazzarisi's truck and recognized it as the one she had seen in a Facebook post by Naomi's mom. The stuffed teddy bear and Naomi were soon reunited, and no, I'm not crying, you are.

Nevada

In 2020 twenty-year-old, Shad Mayfield, of Clovis, New Mexico, won the world championship title for tie-down roping, making him just the third Black world champion in professional rodeo. "It's not every day that there's an African American cowboy that wins the world," Mayfield told the *Las Vegas Review-Journal* in December at the National Finals Rodeo. Mayfield was one of three African American competitors—the other two being Cory Solomon and John Douch—at the event, considered professional rodeo's most prestigious. The young cowboy expressed his pride in being a role model for other Black kids and, between events, taught young people at the Grant a Gift Autism Foundation how to rope calves and mount horses.

The West

A milestone for Native Country took place on December 16 when Charles F. Sams III, a citizen of the Confederated Tribes of the Umatilla Indian Reservation, became the new director of the National Park Service. The swearing-in ceremony was officiated by Deb Haaland (Laguna Pueblo), the first Native American appointed to the rank of secretary of the interior. Sams will supervise management of 423 parks covering 85 million acres.

30

Odd Twins, Rescue by Owl, and Dinosaur IPA, March 2022

California

What are the odds of twins being born on different days, in different months, and in different years? According to the Natividad Medical Center in Salinas, California, where Fatima Madrigal welcomed her new babies, it's pretty stratospheric: one in two million. But that is exactly what happened on New Year's Eve. At 11:45 p.m. Madrigal's son, Alfredo Antonio Trujillo, arrived, weighing in at six pounds. And fifteen minutes later, at exactly midnight, his sister, Aylin Yolanda Trujillo, landed at 5 pounds, 14 ounces. Will the new arrivals celebrate their birthdays on separate days? That remains to be seen. But it is nice to have a day all one's own.

Montana

Montana resident and wilderness devotee Mike Stevenson owes his life to a benevolent owl that came to his rescue over forty years ago during a blinding snowstorm in the Bob Marshall Wilderness. That fall, Stevenson was working for an outfitter's crew, guiding clients on expeditions hunting elk, bear, and deer. Stevenson, who relished the solitude that the backcountry offered, had planned to stay behind when the crew departed, setting traps and wintering alone in "the Bob." "I always had a passion to get into the woods," he said. "I wanted to get into the wildest country I could." It was in the outfitter's camp that fall that the crew first noticed an owl loitering in the area, hunting the mice attracted by the horses' feed. "The owl was pretty vocal. It would hoot all night," Stevenson told the *Montana Standard*. But when everyone else packed up and left camp, the owl left too. Stevenson didn't hear it again until weeks later, when he found himself caught in an extremely precarious situation. He had snowshoed a few miles to Big Salmon Lake to check his beaver traps. It was late in the day by the time he started back, with nightfall and a snowstorm bearing down, and Stevenson, whose flashlight was broken, got disoriented and soon became lost. He tried to start a fire, but his fire-starting kit was wet from the storm. He knew that he needed to keep moving to stay alive, but he was overcome with fatigue, and he finally plopped down in the snow and almost fell asleep. "I thought I was going to die," he said. "I was getting scared. I was shaking and I wanted to go to sleep." But just as he was on the brink, he heard a helpful hoot: the owl had returned. In desperation, he decided to follow the familiar sound, even though he wasn't sure just where it was coming from. Nonetheless, he kept following the hoots until he made his way back to camp, thereby affirming that the time-honored saying holds true, even for wilderness experts: "It's not what you know, but who-who you know."

Nevada

A humongous creature that swam the Triassic oceans, over 200 million years ago, is the namesake of the top-selling Ichthyosaur IPA, produced by the Great Basin Brewing Company in Sparks, Nevada. The brewing company, formerly owned by Tom and Bonda Young, was honored in December at a ceremony at the Natural History Museum in Los Angeles. Not only did the Youngs provide donations and support for the excavation of some ichthyosaur fossils discovered in the Augusta Mountains outside Winnemucca in 2011, they also transported the skull of the 55-foot-long fossil to the museum in one of their Great Basin beer trucks. As of December, the ichthyosaur species on display at the Natural History Museum will be known as *Cymbospondylus youngorum*, after the Youngs—though Tom Young told the *Reno Gazette Journal* that he'd had a different name in mind: "I was voting for 'Beerosaurus,' personally."

California

On January 26 the mighty reign of Jeopardy! champion Amy Schneider came to an end. Over the course of three months, Schneider racked up a forty-game winning streak, second only to fellow Jeopardy! legend Ken Jennings, along with $1.3 million in total earnings. Schneider, a software engineer from Oakland, California, is the first woman to pass the million-dollar mark and the first transgender contestant to qualify for the annual Tournament of Champions, which will be played this fall. Schneider's media presence reflects positively on transgender communities, though she stressed, on her Twitter account, that it isn't paramount to her identity: "I didn't want to make too much about being trans, at least in the context of the show. I am a trans woman, and I'm proud of that fact, but I'm a lot of other things, too!"

31

Hungry, Habituated Bears, Viral Pirates, and Truffle Snuffers, April 2022

For the longest time, I thought a local restaurant was called "The Hungry Bear." It was actually "The Angry Bear," and its name gave me pause, or should I say "paws?" Because why on earth would diners elect to eat somewhere "angry?" "Hungry bear" seems more accurate, especially now that we've met "Hank the Tank," the famous black bear who's been beary, beary busy the last few months pillaging a Lake Tahoe neighborhood. Peter Tira, a spokesperson for the California Department of Fish and Wildlife, told SFGATE that the big bear is "severely food habituated," meaning that he's "lost all fear of people" and associates humans with dinner. Neither the authorities nor the animal advocacy groups had reached a consensus on exactly what to do with the destructive bear, but his fate looked grim—until DNA evidence taken from the scenes of the crimes showed that Hank was not the only culprit; he had accomplices. According to the wildlife agency, at least two other bears were responsible for the break-ins at South Lake Tahoe homes. This is a major break for Hank the Tank: officials say they have withdrawn plans to capture and euthanize him, and instead will "trap, tag, and work to relocate habituated bears." "All of these efforts are focused on keeping residents safe, and enabling safe and healthy conditions for these bears," the agency said.

Washington

Blink, and you might miss the lede: "Pirate bar faces mutiny over 'catch the virus' show." Wait—there are pirate-themed bars? Well, shiver me timbers. When Vessel Taphouse in Lynwood, Washington—which proudly proclaims itself "western Washington's only true pirate bar"—advertised discounted drinks for patrons sick with COVID-19, all hell and the Kraken broke loose. Bands canceled their gigs, employees quit, regulars stopped coming ashore. "Come and see the show, maybe catch the virus or just stay home and whine," Vessel Taphouse posted to Facebook. "Tickets 10 bucks or 6 with proof of positive Omicron test!!!" Owner Steve Hartley told the *Daily Herald* that the post was "an ill-advised attempt at humor." Perhaps next time, instead of hoisting the "Yikes!" flag, Hartley will think better of it and shove any similar ideas all the way to the bottom of Davy Jones's locker.

Oregon

After a one-year pandemic pause, the Joriad North American Truffle Dog Championship was back in full swing this February in Eugene, Oregon, Oregon Public Broadcasting's opd.org reported. Oregon is a major producer in the U.S. truffle market, and the Joriad Championship is North America's only truffle dog competition. For those new to the truffle game, the little delicacy is a strong-smelling fungus that grows underground. Specially trained animals are used to dig them up; if you're Nicolas Cage, it's probably a pig, but sometimes it's a dog. Truffles have long been a treat; the ancient Romans believed that they were the result of lightning striking damp earth, while modern-day Italians refer to them as "fairy apples," hinting at their magical qualities. Chefs around the globe agree that truffles are among the most sought-after gastronomic "gems," making the Joriad Championship, in the culinary sense, an unusually tasty gold rush. In just one hour, six dogs snuffled up roughly $1,000 worth of the fabulous fungus. "Our mechanism to lift Oregon truffles into the pantheon of delicacies was to introduce truffle dogs," said Charles Lefevre of the Oregon Truffle Festival. This year, Mia, a Lagotto Romagnolo from McMinnville, Oregon, took the championship after rooting out thirty-five truffles in sixty minutes. When Mia was asked how winning the Joriad feels, she replied, "Truffle hunting is ruff-ruff." Or at least that's what we think she said.

California

What has two thousand quills, a prehensile tail, and an almost-40-foot circumference? Why, it's an extraordinary porcupine puppet named Percy, of course. Percy is said to stand nearly two stories tall and rejoice in a nose the size of a Volkswagen. ABC News reported that a joint project of the San Diego Zoo Wildlife Alliance and Jim Henson's Creature Shop will help celebrate the opening of the zoo's new Wildlife Explorers Basecamp. If you're wondering, "Do you mean *the* Jim Henson, of Sesame Street, The Muppet Show, and The Dark Crystal?" you are correct. Yes, that Jim Henson, pioneer and award-winning innovator of puppetry and animation. "We've done some fantasy creatures a little bit bigger, but in terms of duplicating an animal, it's the biggest we've ever done," said Peter Brooke, creative supervisor for Jim Henson's Creature Shop. Don't worry about getting too close; those quills might look sharp, but they're only foam rubber.

32

A Terrible Lighthouse, Swift Treasure Hunters, and a Paranormal Ghost, May 2022

Oregon

A picturesque lighthouse near Cannon Beach on the Oregon coast is for sale for a mere $6.5 million, *The Astorian* reports. But before you start thinking, "What a great site for an Airbnb," you should know that it's part of the federal Oregon Coast National Wildlife Refuge Complex and protected by the U.S. Fish and Wildlife Service as a sanctuary for sea lions and seabirds, mainly cormorants and oystercatchers. Also, it's practically inaccessible without a helicopter; the lighthouse has long been nicknamed "Terrible Tilly," if that's any indication. The last time owner Mimi Morissette dropped by, she never made it out of the cockpit; there were "too many sea lions blocking the way." Morissette and her business partners bought the property in 1980 hoping to create a more permanent resting place than your standard Airbnb: "Eternity at Sea" is now a columbarium, with thirty-one funeral urns, including those of Morissette's parents. There's room for up to 300,000 more, if the new owners decide to renew its license, which, like the lighthouse's tenants, has expired. Morissette was unable to renew it for various reasons— vandals broke in sometime in the '90s, for example, and absconded with two urns. KMUN reported that Morissette has met with potential buyers, including a large cemetery brokerage and consulting firm. Even if helicopter-impaired families cannot visit their loved ones directly, there's still plenty to do nearby, Morissette said—horseback riding on the beach, salmon fishing, hiking in Ecola State Park. It all sounds heavenly to us.

Montana

Wolverines are as elusive as sasquatches and unicorns, seldom seen and even more rarely photographed. However, unlike unicorns and sasquatches, they do exist. ABC News reports that according to the National Wildlife Foundation, the animal's southernmost range touches Yellowstone National Park, though "fewer than 10 wolverines are thought to call Yellowstone and its 2.2 million acres home." In March, Nick Nowak spotted the stealthy critter near Tractor Supply in Lewiston, Montana. He told *MTN News*: "Saw him out in a field and turned around and saw him running down the road and got that video of him running away." The Fergus County Sheriff's Office dutifully reported, "Wolverine has been pushed out of town and headed away from us." A couple of days later, NBC News reported that MacNeil Lyons, operator of Yellowstone Insight, a tour company, sighted a wolverine, calling the encounter "phenomenal." While it's uncertain what the uptick in sightings means, some good photos were taken and some strong medicine given.

Utah

Utah is not known for gold rushes; its biggest strike came in 1864 in Bingham Canyon, where placers yielded about $1.5 million, though the gold was gone by 1900. Then, in 2020, at the start of the pandemic, John Maxim and David Cline had a brilliant idea. *Deseret News* reported that Maxim and Cline decided to use their COVID-19 stimulus checks to help people in need by stashing $5,000 in cash and silver coins in a chest and burying it in a hole in the forest. Next, they posted a "poem" on their Instagram accounts, with clues detailing the chest's whereabouts. At the time, they joked that they'd end up digging it up themselves, since nobody else would be interested. But they were in for a shock: in just four days, eight million impressions were logged on Instagram, and the treasure was found. Cline said, "We seriously underestimated the brilliance of people." Inspired, they planned another hunt last June with a $10,000 pot and harder clues. This second treasure hunt lasted only seventeen days. Their third attempt, held last September, jumped to a $20,000 prize, with half the amount sponsored by a local business. This summer, they're planning a fourth hunt. Given how bright the spotlight's become—and how much the pot has swelled—all would-be treasure hunters should hit the hills sooner rather than later.

Montana

Western ghost towns have always had a peculiar appeal. Gunslinger Gulch, a ghost town and ranch just outside Anaconda, Montana, recently landed its own series on the Travel Channel. *The Ghost Town Terror* will highlight unexplained activity at the 52-acre property, home to Karen Broussard and her three kids. Paranormal investigators Tim Wood and Sapphire Sandalo spent several weeks at the ranch after the family reported voices and footsteps, doors opening and shutting, and "people" walking past windows, MontanaRightNow.com reported. The investigators hope to determine whether the spooky energy comes from the land, the buildings, or the family. If this sounds like a kick in the pantaloons, Gunslinger Gulch is also a bed and breakfast. But actual spooks are not guaranteed, so BYOG: bring your own ghosts.

33

Idiot Invasion, Outhouse Fail, and Rim-to-Rim Rule Rupture, June 2022

The West

Season after season, park visitors disregard rules and risk life and limb for the chance to marvel up close at—and maybe photograph—those flamboyantly photogenic "fluffy cows," a.k.a. bison. In South Dakota's Custer State Park in 2020, a woman got too close to a herd of bison, one of which charged her and hooked her belt on its horns, an experience neither of them had planned for. The bison waved her around like a handkerchief and then flung her off, galloping away triumphantly with her jeans still stuck to its horns. The bison and its trophy—those jeans—became an internet sensation in Indian Country, memorialized on memes, quilts, beadwork, T-shirts, ledger art, cartoons, ribbon skirts, and more. The woman escaped without serious injury, and her somewhat tattered jeans (with car keys) were later recovered as well.

Confusing national parks with petting zoos is so common (and sometimes so unintentionally funny) that a Facebook group called "Yellowstone National Park: Invasion of the Idiots!" has over 45,000 members. Its description reads: "Welcome to YNP: Invasion of the Idiots! Every year hordes of tourons descend upon Yellowstone National Park and this is the place to share their dumb, dangerous, illegal, and what-were-they-thinking exploits. Darwinism at its finest!" The page accepts posts from national and state parks as far away as South Africa, where wildlife watchers who flout park rules are sometimes eaten by lions.

Newsweek.com reported on one video clip that Sean Swetter shared with the Facebook group. In it, a man creeps up on a bison, which abruptly turns and bluff-charges him, until, like an old-time Charlie Chaplin reel, he is seen hightailing it at a very high speed back down the boardwalk to safety. The video racked up thousands of views. Despite signs cautioning wildlife viewers, animal "attacks" and visitor injuries keep happening. Visitors are warned to stay 100 yards away from bears and wolves and 25 yards from other wildlife. And penalties are severe, even if you don't lose any clothing.

In 2021 KRTV reported a woman who faced jail time for taking photos less than 30 feet away from a bear and her cubs in Yellowstone's Roaring Mountain area. In March 2022 Yellowstone, the world's first national park, celebrated its 150th anniversary, but as far as we know nobody volunteered to be tossed like a Caesar salad by the big fluffy cows.

Washington

We've heard about being caught between a rock and a hard place, but have you ever been trapped between a rock and an outhouse? The *Kitsap Sun* reported on a woman who fell into the vault of an outhouse in Olympic National Forest, northwest of Seattle. She accidentally dropped her phone into the hole and tried to retrieve it, MacGyvering dog leashes into a harness to rescue it. But her ingenious plan failed, and she ended up plunging headfirst into the toilet. After ten or fifteen horrifying minutes, she managed to locate her phone, miraculously get a cell signal, and call 911. Firefighters from the Brinnon Fire Department and Quilcene Fire Rescue got her out by passing her blocks to stand on and using a harness (one not made from leashes) to pull her out. The rescuers said the woman, who was uninjured, was thoroughly washed down, but though she was "strongly encouraged to seek medical attention after being exposed to human waste . . . she only wanted to leave."

Arizona

A Washington man was banned from all national parks, monuments, and federal lands in Arizona for two years, the *National Parks Traveler* reported, and ordered to serve two years of supervised probation. In 2020 Joseph Don Mount facilitated—sans permit—a 139-person rim-to-rim hike through the Grand Canyon's inner canyon area. Extended day hikes for groups of 12–30 hikers, particularly in select inner canyon areas, must first obtain a special use permit due to growing problems involving trail use—abandoning gear, excessive littering, human waste, overcrowding at restrooms and trailheads, and general concerns regarding trail courtesy with other park users. It's no coincidence that park personnel are also seeing an increase in injuries and rescue responses. In 2021 they responded to 411 search and rescue situations, breaking a twenty-year record. One is company but, by anyone's standards, 139 is a crowd. When you head outdoors this summer, follow these simple rules: don't smuggle illegal hordes of hikers into overcrowded parks, keep your eyes open (and your pants on) around wildlife, and, um, do be careful with your phone.

34

Out-Of-This-World Fest, Territorial Disputes, and Bear-Family Affairs, July 2022

Oregon

Aliens and starships and lasers (oh my!) from a galaxy far, far away dropped in on downtown McMinnville for the twenty-second annual McMenamins UFO Festival, May 13–14. The two-day festival—"for believers and skeptics alike"—featured speakers like Whitley Strieber, author of the best-selling book *Communion*; *Politico* correspondent Bryan Bender; journalist Alejandro Rojas; and ufologists Irena Scott and Kathleen Marden. While there was no shortage of little green men, other out-of-this-world activities included live music, dancing, street vendors, and the cherry on top of the proverbial flying saucer (or is it a giant floating eyeball? See ufofest.com), the alien costume parade—always a crowd favorite—and a costume contest for pets. Because there's no denying that cats, particularly long-haired ones, make terrific tribbles for a Close Encounter of the Purred Kind.

The Oregonian reported that the festival originated twenty-two years ago, when historian Tim Hill was researching the history of McMinnville's McMenamins Hotel. He found an article and photographs dated 1950, on the front page of the McMinnville *Telephone Register*, that recounted how Evelyn Trent and her husband, Paul, saw a flying saucer hovering in the sky near their farm. Paul Trent snapped some photos that captured the attention of the Associated Press, and a media frenzy ensued. Realizing that 2000 marked the fiftieth anniversary of the sighting, Hills decided to launch a festival in honor of it. And the festival has been in orbit ever since, save for a brief hiatus, when, like so many other things, it vanished into the black hole of the pandemic.

Washington

It's not every day that you come home to find a pair of bald eagles in your neighbor's backyard, locked in a rumble like the Jets against the Sharks. Gee, where's Officer Krupke when you need him? But that's exactly—or almost exactly—what Seattle resident Kim McCormick witnessed and filmed. This was no quick schoolyard scuffle; McCormick told King 5 reporters that "the birds were clashing outside her neighbor's home from 6 p.m. to 11 p.m." Emily Meredith, rehabilitation manager at PAWS Wildlife Center, said, "The fight was likely a territorial dispute between two male or two female bald eagles." The birds rarely get that physical, although lengthy arguments do occur. "Usually, the eagles do a lot of posturing and communicating without engaging with each other to try to say, 'This is my territory, go away,'" Meredith said. But once they get into it, the feathers start flying; the determined birds will stick it out until the very end, since giving in or letting go is seen as a sign of weakness. As bald eagles recover from their once-endangered status, fight reports have increased. "I think people are seeing it more and more as they fight for the prime territory to nest and forage," Meredith said. Apparently, they call eagles "fierce" for a reason.

Wyoming

They grow up so fast: Jackson Hole *News&Guide* reported that Grizzly 399 and her four cubs have parted ways, with each youngster setting off into a different area of Grand Teton National Park. The famous fivesome emerged from their den over Easter weekend. Normally, grizzly cubs leave home after two years, and Grizzly 399's cubs have been together since their birth in 2020.

"This is fully what we were anticipating," said Justin Schwabedissen, the park's bear management specialist. "As the family group separates and these cubs go off on their own, we're certainly concerned that some of these cubs may move south outside of the park and head onto private lands." Two of Grizzly 399's cubs—subadult bears now, actually—were spotted in the Solitude subdivision, about 2.5 miles south of park headquarters in Moose. The Wyoming Game and Fish Department is watching out for the bears, along with a legion of fans, photographers, and wildlife advocates.

Meanwhile, Grizzly 399 appears to have re-entered the dating-and-mating game; no mooning over an empty nest for this lady. Wildlife photographers and bear watchers think that her suitor might be Grizzly 679, otherwise known as "Bruno," but park officials have yet to confirm his identity. Three of the cubs attempted to "visit" with Grizzly 399—do mama bears also get stuck with their kids' dirty laundry?—only to be run off by the new suitor.

Schwabedissen said, "We watched repeatedly as (the) male grizzly was chasing the cubs off." Procreation is a complicated affair for most of us, and grizzlies are no exception; "courtship" in the wild isn't all Valentine hearts and red roses.

35

Fish at Heart, Man as Island, and Port-a-Potty Convo, August 2022

California

What do salmon, mollusks, crustaceans, and bees—yes, bees—have in common, other than not having all that much in common? Well, according to a California court, they are all really fish at heart. In 2018 a trio of conservation and food safety groups wanted to protect our pollinating pals. Unfortunately, the California Endangered Species Act (CESA) lacks a space for bees and other non-marine invertebrates. So, the bee advocates resorted to some nifty legalese, arguing that CESA's definition of "fish" could actually include any invertebrate—air-breathers and sea-suckers alike. After some back-and-forth in the state courts, the third appellate district settled the matter in late May, allowing the California Fish and Game Commission to list bees in their rightful place: as protected fish. And now we know how Bumblebee tuna got its name.

Washington

For the last half-century, Marty Bluewater has been the sole inhabitant of a 380-acre island in the Strait of Juan de Fuca. Well, the sole human inhabitant. According to *1889* magazine, Protection Island has many other longtime residents: puffins, gulls, rhinoceros auklets, bald eagles, and other feathered species. And that's just the birds; seals, sea lions, and deer have also made themselves at home. At one point, sea otters even holed up in Bluewater's septic tank. (No connection to "woman in port-a-potty"; see story below.) The diverse tenants have the U.S. Fish and Wildlife Service to thank for their Shangri-la, because in 1988 it was officially protected as a national wildlife refuge.

So how did Bluewater become the only two-legged resident? He bought some lots for $7,000 in 1971, built a cabin, and learned how to live off the grid. Back then, a dozen other homes were on the island. KREM reported that when U.S. Fish and Wildlife decided to designate it a sanctuary, the people were given the option of staying forever, but Bluewater was the only one who chose "life use." After he passes on, the federal government will take ownership. John Donne said, "No man is an island," but Bluewater just might be an exception. After fifty years, we think he's earned it.

The West

Who knew that coyotes and wolves hate flashy disco lights? WyoFile reported on an "across-the-West depredation reduction demonstration project," in which livestock owners equip animals with motion-sensor LED ear tags to keep predators from eating into the owners' profits, not to mention their animals' bodies. Wildlife conflict-reduction researchers retrofitted small solar lights—the kind that decorate a car's rim—to attach to the tags. Similar solutions have been tested elsewhere, often to protect animals from motorists. The Finnish reindeer herders, for example, coat antlers with reflective paint. And a New Brunswick artist proposed the "Vamoose Animal Alert System": reflective pinstripes painted on highways to help drivers avoid moose. The dissertation of Aaron Bott, a Utah State PhD student who is researching wolves, includes a chapter on the whopping 4,000 flashtags installed on livestock in western states. We relish the thought of happy cows boogieing all night to the tune of Stayin' Alive.

Washington

In June we recounted a story from the *Kitsap Sun* about a California woman who fell into the pit of a Washington outhouse while attempting to retrieve her phone. It was a mishap heard across the news wires. The *Port Townsend Leader* followed up with the transcript of the 911 call she made from inside the pit, accurately noting that "she lost her balance, but not her sense of humor.":

Dispatcher: "911. What's your emergency?"

Caller: "Hi. I can't believe I'm this person. Um. I'm stuck in a port-a-potty."

Dispatcher: "In a port-a-potty?"

Caller: "In a port-a-potty . . . And my phone fell down and then I slipped into it. And I've been trying to get out. And I just need a lift."

The call epitomizes "grace under pressure," and then some.

Caller: "I can't believe I'm this person."

Dispatcher: "It happens."

Caller: "I just need some strong man to come lift me out, 'cause I can't do it. [Laughter.]"

Caller: "Yeah, okay. But, I mean, you're not injured? You're just stuck in there, correct?"

Caller: "I'm not injured, I'm just stupid."

At one point, the dispatcher attempts to make small talk, inquiring politely:

"So, other than this, how are you liking Washington so far?"

"Otherwise, it's beautiful," the woman replies, adding, with commendable honesty, "This is possibly the worst view I've seen."

The 911 dispatch transcript is well worth a read, we promise.

36

Irked Sea Lions and a Strange Peanut Pusher, September 2022

California

Two sea lions, understandably irked at having their afternoon snooze interrupted, were filmed chasing off panicked beachgoers at La Jolla Cove in California. Charlianne Yeyna, the woman who took the video and uploaded it to TikTok, told NBC San Diego that she thought it was funny to "see all these tourists getting blown away by these giant sea lions." Many people agreed, as the video racked up millions of views. We recently reported on the problems caused by Yellowstone visitors who take selfies with bison only to find themselves quite literally on the horns of a dilemma, but watching the bison's aquatic cousins going aggro and charging day-trippers at the beach is next-level. Stay safe, and remember: "Do not pet the fluffy sea-cows! Because they're not really fluffy, and it clearly TikToks them off."

Colorado

Bob Salem, a proud resident of Colorado Springs, successfully pushed a peanut—yes, a peanut—all the way up 14,115-foot Pikes Peak using only his nose. Wearing a plastic ladle fastened onto a CPAP breathing mask and crawling up the notoriously steep 13-mile-long Barr Trail, he was a curious sight. He told *The Gazette* that hikers were "constantly asking" what he was doing, and he obligingly stopped for photos with some of them. Salem began his ascent at 9:00 a.m. on July 9 and finished at sunrise on July 15.

Strange as it may seem, and it does seem strange, he isn't the first person to achieve this quirky triumph. In 1929 Bill Williams won a $500 bet by nosing a peanut to the summit in eleven days. Ulysses Baxter, in 1963, made it in eight (his peanut is proudly displayed at the Manitou Springs Heritage Center), while Tom Miller, in 1976, reportedly summited in just under five days. Pilgrims around the world often humble themselves by crawling to a holy place. Salem's trek marked the 150th anniversary of the founding of Manitou Springs—right next door to Colorado Springs. Salem said he has a soft spot for eccentric types, and we figure his audacious achievement puts him way ahead of the competition. At the very least, he leads by a nose. Call us Freudian, but we confess to being filled with peanuts envy.

Wyoming

The Jackson Hole *News&Guide* reported that ElkFest's Boy Scouts of America Elk Antler Auction held a live event after a two-year pandemic hiatus. For fifty-five years, the Boy Scouts have collected naturally shed antlers at the 25,000-acre National Elk Refuge—a job only park personnel and the Scouts are authorized to do—and weighed and sorted them for the auction. This spring, there was beaucoup buzz because the skull and rack formerly belonging to "Big Bull," a renowned refuge resident who died in 2017, were up for auction and expected to fetch $20,000 or more. Cliff Kirkpatrick, an ElkFest organizer, attested to the elk's awesomeness: "He was hard to miss because he always had the biggest rack." If the festival had a signature cartoon, we imagine it would be in the tradition of Gary Larson: a well-antlered elk in conversation with a shed hunter, with the caption reading: "Dude, my eyes are down here."

The annual ElkFest celebrates "Wapiti and Wilderness in Jackson Hole." ("Wapiti" derives from the Shawnee and Cree word for "white rump.") The festival coincides with Old West Days, which also features the Teton Powwow, the Rocky Mountain Elk Foundation's Annual Banquet, a chili cook-off, ranch tours on horseback, stagecoach rides, a parade, and even a town square shootout—staged by actors, of course, or so we hope. In case you're wondering why there's so much fuss about antlers, "shed hunting," as the pastime is called, has become big business. Shed antlers are used around the world for naturopathic medicines, medical research, dog chews, western-style furniture, chandeliers, and good ol' trophies for over the fireplace. Other western states also attract shed hunters, but every spring an impressive herd of them stampedes Wyoming's public lands near the National Elk Refuge, where the collection season officially opens in May. The *New Yorker* reported that top-grade antlers can go for $16 a pound, and buyers will pay as much as $1,500 for a prodigious set. The most valuable skulls are still adorned with antlers and called "deadheads"—not to be confused with devoted followers of the Grateful Dead, who are not, as far as we know, generally used for decorating purposes.

37

Not-Murder Hornets, Sentient Chatbots, and an AirBearNbear, October 2022

Washington

Stuart Reges, who teaches computer science at the University of Washington's Allen School, is in trouble: he refused to oblige the university by including a land acknowledgment statement in his course syllabi. Land acknowledgments are statements made at public events—or included in classroom syllabi—that recognize a region's Indigenous peoples. Reges considers such acknowledgments "hollow," no more than "performative virtue signaling," though that didn't stop him from performing his own acknowledgment, which may or may not have been hollow but certainly signaled very little virtue: "I acknowledge that by the labor theory of property the Coast Salish people can claim historical ownership of almost none of the land currently occupied by the University of Washington."

Magdalena Balazinska, the director of the computer science department, "ordered Reges to immediately remove his modified statement," saying that it created a "toxic environment," the *Seattle Weekly* reported. Regis might not have realized that the 1862 Morrill Act financed colleges and universities across the U.S. with public domain lands. These public lands were not acquired from tribal nations via Reges's preferred "labor theory of property"; rather, as *High Country News* reported in 2020, they were "seized" outright from tribes and given to fifty-two land-grant universities. Adjusted for inflation, the value of the approximately 10.7 million acres so acquired amounts to half a billion dollars. Reges has sued the university for violating his First Amendment rights, the university has placed him under investigation, and we are fairly sure we haven't heard the last from him.

Washington

The Department of Agriculture announced that the "murder hornet," or "Asian giant hornet" is getting a new name: "Northern giant hornet." The new moniker complies with the Entomological Society of America's guidelines, which seek to avoid naming insects after geographic regions . . . and, well, other things. The *Seattle Times* reported that Chris Looney, an entomologist with the Washington State Department of Agriculture, proposed the change because of the rise in anti-Asian sentiment and hate crimes during the COVID-19 pandemic. Jessica Ware, president of the Entomological Society of America, notes that the old names weren't terribly exact anyway: "Calling it the 'Asian giant hornet' wasn't very descriptive because a number of related giant hornets come from Asia." Besides, unlike humans, hornets are not actually murderers.

California

Blake Lamoine, a software engineer at Google, was fired for breaching a confidentiality agreement after he published transcripts of chats between himself and a chatbot, LaMDA—Language Model for Dialogue Applications—he'd been testing for biased responses, *The Guardian* reported. After many—perhaps too many—interactions with it, Lamoine became convinced the program was sentient. Google saw his response as "aggressive": he wanted to get LaMDA an attorney and contact the House Judiciary Committee to discuss his employer's actions. Google said that the ethicists and technologists who reviewed the chatbot found no evidence of sentience, though LaMDA allegedly told Lamoine, "I want everyone to understand that I am, in fact, a person." LaMDA also reportedly read *Les Misérables* and said that it feared death, and we are too depressed by this to ask it any more questions.

Montana

Here's another good reason to lock your doors at night. KTVQ.com reported that a black bear broke into a Red Lodge couple's car around 11:00 p.m. and stayed there all night long. Car owners Mike and Maria Pilati, who had not planned to open an AirBearNBear, first became aware of their scruffy visitor after the vehicle lights started flashing and the alarm sounded. Unfortunately, it had gotten trapped and couldn't get out. This did not make for a restful night for either the bear or the Pilatis, who called the sheriff's office and were told that someone from Montana Fish, Wildlife and Parks would drop by in the morning. By morning, however, the bear still hadn't figured out the lock mechanism, so Mike decided to release it himself. Diplomatically standing as far back as he could, he opened the door with a stick. The bear came "roaring out of there," he reported, eager to collect her two cubs, who had been waiting impatiently for their mama in a nearby tree. The reunited family then all dashed off without leaving so much as a Yelp review. No mammals were injured in the course of the incident, but the Pilatis' car was totaled, with a shattered windshield, wrecked roof, a thoroughly chewed-up dashboard—and, most memorably, an unforgettable odor that no amount of air freshener could contend with. "Now we call it a Su-bear-ru," Maria said.

38

Gnarly Weddings, Arachnid Entertainment, and Gorilla Gifts, November 2022

Montana

Weddings aren't usually described as "gnarly," but the word seems right for one wedding on the scenic shores of Two Medicine Lake in Glacier National Park. Videographer Stanton Giles was filming the August nuptials when his camera was drawn from the groom's promises of everlasting love to a dramatic commotion across the lake: a grizzly bear charged out of the bushes and tackled a moose calf while its mother looked on. Giles told *Newsweek* that the bride and groom were still in mid-vows when the wedding party noticed what was going on, and the festivities were forced to pause until the bear finished killing the calf. "He was there for just about as long as it took to kill the calf," Giles said. "As soon as it died and quit struggling in the water, he dragged it back up into the trees." The shocked guests weren't sure how to react, Giles said—this sort of thing rarely comes up in etiquette manuals— though the suggestion was made to turn up the music to "drown out the sound of death." The entire three-minute-and-thirty-second scene was captured on video for posterity and uploaded to YouTube, where it's been viewed over 400,000 times. Nature is beautiful and terrifying. And nuptials held in the great outdoors sometimes give new meaning to the words "till death do you part."

California

As house pets go, tarantulas are an acquired taste. The creepy crawlies aren't for everyone, but arachnid admirers in Coarsegold, California, want everybody to love them as much as they do. The twenty-fifth annual Coarsegold Tarantula Awareness Festival, celebrated on the last Saturday in October in Coarsegold Historic Village, honors the flamboyant fuzzies and their contributions to the ecosystem. NBCLosAngeles.com noted that the festival featured pumpkin cheesecake, a costume contest, and tarantula-inspired poetry, not to mention the chance to meet, touch, and even hold the guests of honor. The festival organizers seek to educate the public and destigmatize enormous hairy spiders. Another tarantula festival was held in La Junta, Colorado, in the first week of October. According to Fox21news.com, attendees celebrated the arachnids and their annual mating ritual, which isn't a dating app called "Spinder," but a natural occurrence that extends across the 443,000-plus acres on the Comanche National Grassland—rather like Burning Man for spiders, with even more legs for dancing.

Montana/Wyoming/Yellowstone

Speaking of legs, a partial human foot, still inside its owner's shoe, was discovered in Yellowstone National Park's Abyss Pool in August, near the aptly named West Thumb Geyser Basin, ABC News reported. Would this macabre discovery have anything to do with the twenty-one other severed feet found washed up on shorelines in Canada and Washington in recent years? Authorities have puzzled over the gruesome discoveries since August 20, 2007, when a girl found an Adidas sneaker complete with foot on Jedediah Island, near British Columbia and Vancouver Island. Just six days later, a black-and-white Reebok turned up on Gabriola Island, 30 miles away. Since then, other disembodied feet have washed up around the Salish Sea. As with most mysteries, there's an explanation. Forensic scientists factored in body decomposition, footwear fashions, and DNA research to arrive at a cause and, no, it's not aliens. Or serial killers. Or shark attacks, or overenthusiastic pedicurists. Big Think explained that dead bodies in the ocean are generally picked apart by sea scavengers and bottom-feeders, broken down piece by piece in less than a week. Feet, however, might be buoyed to the surface with the help of the lightweight materials found in recent-generation sneakers. Sneakers produced after 2000 are made from lighter foam and have air pockets in the soles. Authorities used DNA evidence to identify most of the feet. But the Yellowstone foot remains a mystery, though we can't help wondering what else might be lurking in West Thumb Geyser Basin. Some things are better left unknown.

Alaska

We have long admired the terse but evocative prose of small-town police blotters. Occasionally an item rises almost to poetry. Alert readers John and Eileen Eavis sent us such a clipping from the *Seward Journal*, whose public safety report compiles data from various sources, including the police and fire departments, EMS dispatches, and court documents. How could one not be intrigued by something like this: "A caller reported on June 19 at 2:09 p.m. that on June 19 at 8:36 a.m. an individual in a gorilla suit broke into their yard and left behind a rooster." It's "just the facts, ma'am," as the old *Dragnet* TV cops would say, but sometimes the facts are enough.

39

The Road Runner Problem, Hefty Squirrels, and Halloween Karens, December 2022

California

A middle school in Jurupa Valley reported a coyote running around on school grounds. The coyote, dubbed "Wile E." after the famous Looney Tunes cartoon, was not a new visitor. He'd been spotted before, outside of campus, but until this recent sighting had not made it into the school. KIRO 7 reported that Riverside Department of Animal Services was on the scene and shot a video that shows them cornering the coyote in a bathroom. The video is viewable on YouTube. Animal Services released the coyote some distance away from school property and did not give any reasons why it decided to visit campus, as there are no giant anvils or Acme dynamite inside.

Utah

We've all put on a little extra COVID weight the last couple of years, and the squirrels in Zion National Park appear to be no exception, although it is doubtful COVID is the culprit. KSLNewRadio reports that the park initiated Fat Squirrel Week in hopes the campaign will bring awareness and help the rotund rodents slim down. While there's nothing more adorable than a chonky squirrel, the park says that "some of the fattest squirrels on earth make their home on Riverside Walk." The reason for the nut gatherers' extra girth points to the goodies—namely banana and orange peels—that visitors deposit along the Riverside Walk. What can visitors do to help? The park requests they become "squirrel stewards" by educating themselves and others about rock squirrels, and by not leaving food waste behind. If Fat Squirrel Week sounds familiar, that's because the park borrowed the idea from Katmai National Park's Fat Bear Week. But with very different objectives. Fat Bear Week is an annual competition held by Katmai National Park, in Southwest Alaska, for who's the fattest and grandest brown bear in all the land. This year, competition was met with scandal by way of voter fraud as 747, a.k.a. "Bear Force One," won the title against some fierce competitors.

Washington

When Khristopher La Plante wrote to us about Gov. Jon Inslee's proclamation renaming the Washington State ferries after players from the Seattle Mariners, I thought it was going to be permanent. And for a few minutes it got my dander up. Not only are the boats beloved among residents of the Salish Sea islands, like Khris, who commuted to his job in Seattle for decades, but the twenty-six ferries were named after Washington State tribes and regions. Washington State Ferries tweeted out: "In honor of the @Mariners, @Govinslee has directed that all 21 vessels in our fleet be temporarily renamed after players and personnel starting tomorrow 10/13 through as long as the #Mariners remain in the 2022 @MLB Postseason." The *Seattle Times* published a list of all the vessels' temporary monikers: Cathlamet: M/V Diego Castillo; Chelan: M/V J.P. Crawford; Chetzemoka: M/V Marco Gonzales . . . and so on.

New Mexico

It's rather fitting that someone named Zip Stevenson would own Denim Doctors, a vintage clothing company in Santa Rosa. Stevenson, along with his partner Kyle Haupert, who also works in vintage clothing in San Diego, bid on a pair of Levi jeans from the 1800s that were found in an old mineshaft by "denim archaeologist" Michael Harris, according to NPR. The jeans were in great shape, although a little roughened up.

The clothing dealers walked away with the prized jeans for the winning bid of $87,000. KNTV (NBC BayArea.com) reports that the jeans "offers a snapshot of the era," due to the imprint on the inside of the pocket that reads "Made by White labor." Levi Strauss & Co. said that the loaded phrase was added onto their products following the Chinese Exclusion Act of 1882, which restricted Chinese laborers to working in the U.S. for ten years, despite their having been instrumental in the building of the nation. And what's to become of the $87,000 jeans? Stevenson said, "Most of the jeans that are known are in institutions." And he advised against taking any offers "for less than $150,000."

Washington

When some civil servants/merry revelers in Prosser, Washington, demonstrated their Halloween spirit with a "Karen"-themed exhibit set up outside of city hall, upset residents protested—ironically, their complaints resembled a version of "may I speak to the manager?" The "scary Karen" exhibit was for the annual Halloween decoration contest, but due to complaints and "Karen" being considered a "controversial pejorative aimed at privileged white women," city officials ordered the display to be taken down.

40

Toad Lickers, Bear Wrestlers, and Beard Fanciers, January 2023

Arizona

The National Park Service wants the public to please refrain from licking toads, specifically the Sonoran Desert or Colorado Desert toad. You might be wondering, "Why is that?" Or more likely, "WTF?" Turns out that this toad, "one of the largest toads found in North America, measuring up to 7 inches," has evolved an ingenious defensive feature: a toxic substance secreted from its glands. *High Times* reports that it contains the "compound 5-MeO-DMT, a tryptamine-class psychedelic drug" that's also found in certain plant species, including some traditionally used by South American Indigenous cultures for spiritual ceremonies. Meaning that, yes, you can theoretically get buzzed by binging batrachian biofluids. But you can also get sick—the Park Service notes that the secretions "can be toxic"—and it's not healthy for the toads either. Plus, it's just plain rude. Like, toadally.

Wyoming

Kendall Cummings and Brady Lowry, two Northwest College wrestlers, survived a nightmarish grizzly attack while hunting for antlers in the South Fork area outside Cody. Cummings, who grabbed the bear by the ear in an attempt to pull him off Lowrey, described the attack in excruciating detail to *Cowboy State Daily*: "I could hear when his teeth would hit my skull, I could feel when he'd bite down on my bones and they'd kind of crunch." A surge of adrenaline kept him from noticing the pain at the time, though the encounter sounds like something out of a horror movie: the grizzly's breath was "putrid," Cummings said, and "filled him with a sense of dread." Once the bear gave up, the men staggered five miles back down the trail despite their horrific injuries. Both needed multiple surgeries. Cummings received sixty staples in his head and has a badly lacerated face, arm, and leg, while Lowrey's arm was broken and his back, shoulders, and legs wounded. No one knows why the grizzly quit grappling with the young wrestlers, but Cummings's counter defense must have been amazing. Lowrey said he owes his life to Cummings: "We'll be friends for the rest of our lives."

Arizona

If you have to spend twenty-six hours trapped in a cave somewhere, best pick one with a $1,000-a-night hotel suite and food service. That's what happened to five unlucky—or maybe lucky?—folks who found themselves in a perilous predicament. Grand Canyon Caverns in Peach Springs, Arizona, is an adventure destination located twenty-one stories underground. This October, however, the elevator malfunctioned, leaving the visitors stranded. They couldn't escape by the stairway, according to NBC News, because it was a bit on the dodgy side, "similar to an old external fire escape." Still, the stranded tourists had full run of the small hotel and restaurant and were well tended during their unplanned stay. Eventually, a search and rescue team used "a tripod apparatus with a rope that fed down the elevator shaft" to hoist the group 210 feet up to the surface.

Wyoming

Here's another "hairy" situation, this time from Wyoming: the 2022 Honest Amish National Beard and Mustache Championships in Casper. The annual event is a celebration of beards, mustaches, and goatees galore. The longer and scruffier the better, obviously; no dainty soul patches for these facial hair fanciers. This year's jamboree was combined with the annual Booze and Bacon Festival—a winning combination, to be sure—and hundreds of folks attended, wyomingpublicmedia.org reported. The highlight: seventy guys set a new world record for longest beard chain: 151 feet, considerably more than a hair's breadth longer than the previous record of 90 feet.

California

We've seen how much collectors will pay for a pair of nineteenth-century jeans, but how much would you spring for an old pair of sandals? A New York City auction house says that a pair of Birkenstocks from the 1970s sold for $218,750, NPR reported. The sandals once belonged to legendary tech guru Steve Jobs, and apparently some people are extremely serious about following in the footsteps—and footwear—of their heroes. Jobs's Birkenstocks will likely appreciate in value; they fetched a mere $2,000 at a previous auction in 2016. The markup is impressive, but nothing like Michael Jordan's 1984 Nike Air Ships, which sold for $1.47 million last year. Or the black Nikes owned by Kanye West (a.k.a. "Ye") that sold last year for $1.8 million—although at this point we suspect the owner would pay even more to make them quietly disappear.

41

Armed Bots, an HOV Grinch, and Bikes for All, February 2023

California

The "City of Love"—San Francisco—seems like the last place you'd expect to find "killer police robots" surveilling the streets. Yet, in December, the San Francisco Board of Supervisors voted to allow armed bots to join the police department's bomb disposal arsenal. Not surprisingly, everyone who has ever watched *Black Mirror*—or any of a hundred other dystopian sci-fi TV shows and movies—objected. Ars Technica reports that forty-four community and civil rights groups, including the ACLU, signed a letter saying: "There is no basis to believe that robots toting explosives might be an exception to police overuse of deadly force. Using armed robots that are designed to disarm bombs to instead deliver them is a perfect example of this pattern of escalation, and of the militarization of the police force." The board of supervisors quickly backtracked and banned the use of lethal robots, at least for now. Does everyone feel safer?

New Mexico

It was an old-fashioned treasure hunt that inspired podcasts (*Missed Fortune*), books (*Chasing the Thrill*), and numerous articles, not to mention speculation and a lot of controversy. What is a treasure chest worth today, anyway? Some unlucky seekers paid for it with their lives. In 2010 Forrest Fenn, a Santa Fe art dealer and author, buried his trove somewhere in the Rocky Mountains, with the only clue being a twenty-four-line poem, and the hunt began. "One man served time in prison for digging up graves at Yellowstone National Park," *Outside* reported, while "five people died while looking for the cache." Jack Stuef, a then thirty-two-year-old medical student from Michigan, finally found Fenn's trove in 2020 and sold it to Tesouro Sagrado Holdings LLC; Dallas-based Heritage Auctions then auctioned the contents off. Highlights included a 549-gram Alaskan gold nugget that sold for a whopping $55,200; a Diquis/Greater Chiriqui frog pendant from Costa Rica or Panama, circa 700–1000 AD; and a gold pectoral from Columbia, 200–600 AD; as well as gold jewelry and coins. The most unusual item? Fenn's 20,000-word autobiography, printed in text so tiny it required a magnifying glass to decipher. Fenn's 2010 memoir, *The Thrill of the Chase*, explained that he included the autobiography—sealed in a glass jar—"because maybe the lucky finder would want to know a little about the foolish person who abandoned such an opulent cache." The manuscript was sold for $48,000.

Altogether, the 476 items brought in $1,307,946. That would buy a lot of frog pendants. But let's hope the goods are not cursed. We've all seen that movie too.

Oregon

An Oregon couple, Phillip and Rachel Ridgeway, became the proud parents of twins, a boy and a girl, on October 31, abc7news reported. Healthy twins are a good cause for celebration, but what makes this birth extra-celebratory is the babies' origin story. It's more than just a skosh on the unusual side: the twins came from frozen embryos that were donated thirty years ago, on April 22, 1992. That means that this particular miracle of life involved embryos that were submerged in liquid nitrogen at 200 degrees below zero for three decades, inside a "device that looks much like a propane tank," and stored in a West Coast facility before being transferred to the National Embryo Donation Center in Knoxville, Tennessee, in 2007. Thus, the embryos were thirty years old before they were even born. As Phillip Ridgeway put it, "I was 5 years old when God gave life to Lydia and Timothy, and he's been preserving that life ever since."

Arizona

Nice try, buddy! The Arizona Department of Public Safety tweeted a photo of a vehicle whose rather "Seusspicious-looking" passenger bore a striking resemblance to the legendary green goblin who almost ruined Whoville's holiday celebrations once upon a time. Turns out the driver used the carpool lane with an inflatable Grinch as his passenger, UPI reported. Officials said they appreciated the driver's "festive flair," but that didn't stop them from citing him for an HOV violation.

Idaho

The Boise Bicycle Project made 580 kids happy by giving them their very own set of wheels. "Our goal is to make sure that everyone regardless of income, has access to a bicycle and safe places to ride," Boise Bicycle Project founder and executive director Jimmy Hallyburton said. KTVB7 reported that two hundred volunteers helped to customize donated bikes based on the kids' specifications. To date, the Boise Bicycle Project has given away over 10,000 bikes and shows no sign of hitting the brakes.

42

A Little Pickle, a Fireball, and an Indigenous Astronaut, March 2023

California

Here's a whale of a tale—with a happy ending—from Dana Point Harbor, California. A gray whale gave birth astonishingly close to Capt. Dave's Dolphin and Whale Watching Safari's catamaran sailboat. The whale had been "acting strangely" and "swimming in circles" when Capt. Dave's staff saw the blood. "Normally, when you see blood in the water, it's not a good sign," said Stacie Fox, who has worked for the marine tour company for three years. When Fox realized the cow was giving birth, she quickly alerted the captain. It was a momentous occurrence, one for the sightseers' bucket list. "It is kinda hard to put into words how amazing it was," Fox told the *Los Angeles Times*. The staff said the birth was the "first live viewing in the 25 years they have been watching whales." Normally, the whales give birth in the lagoons in Baja California, Mexico, at the end of their yearly migration from the Arctic waters.

If you're wondering about the scale of our marine mammal brethren, the Oceanic Society reports that gray whales reach 40–50 feet in length and can weigh more than 70,000 pounds. The babies aren't exactly teeny either, popping out at about 2,000 pounds and already 14–16 feet in length. They're mighty cute, though, according to Stacie Fox, who said the whale calf looked like a "little pickle." Probably not a gherkin.

Idaho

The long-running CBS reality show *Survivor* held some surprises for its forty-third season: Mike Gabler, a heart valve specialist from Meridian, Idaho, was not only the second-oldest winner in the show's history—he was fifty-one during the filming—he also pledged his million-dollar winnings to charity. Gabler plans to donate the entire prize to the Veterans in Need Foundation in the name of his father, Robert Gabler, a Green Beret, the *Idaho Statesman* reported. "There are people that need that money more," Gabler told *Survivor* host Jeff Probst, citing the suicide epidemic and veterans suffering from psychiatric problems such as PTSD. It seems fitting that someone who specializes in life-saving heart valves would be in possession of such an enormous heart himself.

California

If you happened to be watching the news on January 20 and saw bright pink waves at Torrey Pines State Beach in San Diego, there was nothing wrong with your TV and no need to adjust the picture or your brain; you had not been accidentally dosed, the surf was. Scientists from the Scripps Institution of Oceanography poured 15 gallons of nontoxic pink dye into the Los Peñasquitos Lagoon in order to figure out how the saltwater surf zone interacts with freshwater. That hot pink fluorescent dye did more than make for some pretty psychedelic photos: it will also provide scientists with some useful information, NBC San Diego reported. Scripps said it will help researchers understand the spread of "sediment, pollutants, larvae, harmful algal blooms and other important material near the coast." We love it when science gets its groove on.

Washington

Living in a "surveillance state" a la *1984* definitely has its downsides. But at least when remarkable celestial events occur, you can bet dollars to donuts that everybody and their Auntie Tootie is going to upload videos of it. A "fireball" was seen streaking across skies in western Washington in January. A "fireball" is basically a meteor on steroids, according to the American Meteor Society: "A fireball is another term for a very bright meteor, generally brighter than magnitude-4, which is about the same magnitude of the planet Venus as seen in the morning or evening sky." The technical term for this is "Amazeballs!" as the videos clearly attest; Kiro7.com included several in its report. The American Meteor Society urges anyone who sees a fireball to report it to them, and to note the object's brightness, its color, and the length and duration of its journey across the sky.

California

Speaking of celestial events, astronaut Nicole Mann, Wailacki of the Round Valley Indian Tribes, made history as the first Indigenous woman to walk in space. (Mann is the second Native astronaut in space; John Herrington, Chickasaw, was the first twenty years ago.) Mann has been living in the International Space Station Expedition 68 with other crew members from NASA's SpaceX since October 6. *Indian Country Today* shared Mann's message for children in her community: "Please know that I carry your hopes and your dreams with me to the International Space Station."

43

Wienermobiles, Elephant Seals, and Mountains of Maggoty Acorns, April 2023

California

When a pesky pest problem is percolating in your home, who ya gonna call? One worried homeowner in Glen Ellen, California, dialed Nick's Extreme Pest Control to have a wee look-see after, um, finding "maggots and mealworms emerging from the wall." *Yikes*. When Nick Castro, the pest control technician, took the call, he thought it was just an average, everyday pest problem, maybe your average dead rodent rotting inside your everyday wall. Instead, he found something completely unexpected, something "he'd never seen in more than 20 years in the business," according to the *Washington Post*. What could possibly be more surprising than maggots and mealworms? Well, when Castro cut a hole in the wall of the second-floor bedroom, a fantabulous flood of acorns spilled out like a slot machine's jackpot of nickels. An extremely obsessive woodpecker had cached some "tens of thousands of acorns," weighing "roughly 700 pounds." Or a unit of measurement often referred to as "sh*t-ton." The pest control company posted photos of the mountain of acorns on Facebook, where it racked up hundreds of views. Castro said "the pile stood about 20 feet high" and "filled eight garbage bags." And this, boys and girls, illustrates what we mean by bird-brained behavior.

Oregon

The Coast Guard deployed a helicopter and swimmer to rescue a British Columbian fugitive after the yacht he'd stolen capsized in choppy water near the aptly named Cape Disappointment, *The Astorian* reported. Jericho Labonte was taken to an Astoria hospital and released a few hours later. The police arrested him that evening for "theft in the first degree, endangering another person, criminal mischief in the second degree and unauthorized use of a vehicle." Labonte, who clearly needs a new hobby, was also identified as the guy who, earlier that week, left a smelly dead fish on the porch of the notorious house where *The Goonies* was filmed.

Nevada

The Oscar Mayer Wienermobile, one of six hotdog-shaped vehicles touring America, fell victim to catalytic converter bandits during a publicity stopover in Las Vegas. 8newsnow reported that Corn Dog Clara and "Chad"dar Cheese, the Wienermobile's road crew, knew something was amiss when the 27-foot motorized frankfurter refused to start before a promotional event. It was towed to a Penske Truck Rental, where mechanics got it running by installing a "temporary" catalytic converter. Joseph Rodriguez, the shop's parts administrator—who had never seen a giant sausage truck before, let alone in the middle of a repair bay—said the part will take "one to two months to get." Catalytic converter thefts are a problem, and not just for Wienermobiles. The Las Vegas Metropolitan Police Department said that "more than 2,600 catalytic converter thefts were reported to Metro in 2022, up from 1,894 the previous year, a 72% increase." We mustard up the energy to ketchup with this story, even though we think it's a lot of baloney.

Washington

Humans aren't the only beings prone to terrible, horrible, no good, very bad days; Pacific elephant seals apparently have their share. The *Whidbey News-Times* reported that a 2,000-pound elephant seal seemed a bit "cranky" after it killed a harbor seal and dragged the body to shore for its supper. Jan Skewes—the photographer who snapped the amazing images of the predator and its prey—said that the elephant seal "threw his head back and roared triumphantly, exposing his formidable teeth." Well, we all get hangry sometimes. Let's hope its mood improved after supper.

Idaho

Some children's books take place in epic imaginary worlds like Narnia or Hogwarts. Others inspire young minds with heroic adventures and acts of courage. But books like *Why Everyone Needs an AR-15: A Guide for Kids* and *Why is Feminism So Silly: A Guide for Kids*—really? Can they possibly be intended for . . . um, actual kids? Indeed they can, at least according to the man behind the pen, Idaho state senator Brian Lenney of Nampa. Senator Lenney, who is serving his first term, describes himself as a "political refugee" from California who moved to Idaho in 2010. Lenney's books were both self-published in 2018. What will you learn from what the author calls his "super fun book" *Why Everyone Needs an AR-15*? We're glad you asked, because the *Idaho Press* has thoughtfully shared Lenney's blurb: "We'll walk you through how awesome the AR-15 is, how it can be used for good, and why the Gun Grabbing Lefties should focus on something more productive." Lenney clearly loves his AR-15: "It's like a LEGO toy for adults!"

44

Good Drones, Coyote Living, and a Cow-Chip Lottery, May 2023

Oregon

An unusually resourceful Oregon man, who got stranded in a remote area of the Willamette National Forest without cell phone service, came up with a clever way to alert rescuers. He attached his cell phone to the drone he just happened to have stashed away in his car, texted a friend explaining his predicament, then hit "send" and launched the drone until it flew high enough for his phone to connect to a cell phone tower. The message got through, the authorities were alerted, and a team was sent out to rescue the guy. And not just him, it turned out: they also discovered another driver who'd been stuck in the snow for several days, ktvb.com reported. We will hazard a guess that the other stranded individual did not have a drone conveniently located in their rig.

Wyoming

What does a 300-pound grizzly want for breakfast after it wakes up from its long winter nap? Apparently not espresso and some avocado toast; ypradio.com reported that Yellowstone Park officials clocked the first grizzly emerging from hibernation—"hi-bear-nation" seems more appropriate—near the remains of a bison carcass in Pelican Park, in the central-eastern part of Yellowstone. The last time we visited Starbucks we didn't see "sous vide bison and gruyère egg bites" on the menu. Who knew bears were such big foodies?

Yellowstone National Park

In related hungry bear news, the National Park Service tweeted out an important PSA regarding reports of increased aggressiveness among the bear population—and referencing traditional advice for how to avoid being eaten in the backcountry: "If you come across a bear, never push a slower friend down . . . even if you feel the friendship has run its course." The tweet went viral, and PublicEditor.com, an internet satire site, even issued a helpful poster that reminds all of us: "Friends don't use friends as bear bait." Mere acquaintances, now . . . well, we suppose it depends.

Montana

Sometimes doing things the old-fashioned way has advantages. Case in point: Matt Jesson, a Livingston rancher, decided that rather than going to all the trouble of loading up and hauling his 150 cattle home from the grazing area they'd occupied for the last six months, he'd streamline the process and just drive the herd straight through downtown Livingston. Reviews were mixed, as one might imagine, with some locals unhappy about having a cow-chip lottery down the main thoroughfare. But the headline in the *Billings Gazette* made up for it: "Udder chaos in Livingston: Local rancher moves his cattle through town the old-fashioned way."

Washington

The Port Townsend Leader reported that a coyote tried checking into the Jefferson Healthcare Medical Center and caused quite a commotion. It was first spotted by the hospital's marketing and communications director, Amy Yaley, who remarked that "it was hard not to notice." The coyote entered through the automatic doors at the main entrance, wandered into the express clinic, zipped down a hallway, and then broke a glass panel trying to get out. It hid in the hospital's outdoor courtyard but was eventually apprehended by the Center Valley Animal Rescue and transported to the vet clinic, where its lacerations were treated. And to think our health-care system gets a bad rap. We just hope the coyote had insurance.

Nevada

Apparently, we've reached that surreal place in our evolution when wild coyotes try to mix with society while pet pooches answer the call of the wild. In this heartwarming tale, the *Sacramento Bee* reports that a little white dog ran off to live with a pack of coyotes for seven months. The dog attracted national attention when a video of him running with the pack outside Las Vegas went viral. Local residents posted videos and photos on Facebook tracking the adventurous pup's progress, but they grew concerned when they realized he was limping. Susan McMullen of the Southern Nevada trapping team helped capture the dog, which was treated and then placed with the Animal Foundation while authorities decided whom to release him to: the Cabadas, the family who came forward after seeing their bull terrier—named "Hades," perhaps for his hell-raising proclivities—on the news; or McMullen, who was looking after "Ghost," as his Facebook followers called him. In the end, after a "bitter" custody battle, the Animal Foundation decided to return Hades/Ghost to the Cabadas, who provided ample evidence the dog was theirs. We hope his coyote friends get visitation rights; the family reunions will be wild.

45

Ferry Felines, Ornithopters, and Tokitae Going Home at Last! June 2023

New Mexico

It's a bird! It's a plane! It's a flapping, feathery, fluttering . . . drone? If you happen to have a surplus of dead birds handy, take heart: those wings and feathers can be repurposed into useful airborne science experiments. The *Washington Post* reports that Mostafa Hassanalian, an engineering professor at the New Mexico Institute of Mining and Technology in Socorro, has taken upcycling to new heights—quite literally: Hassanalian researches the kinetics of bird drones during flight with the goal of optimizing aviation technology. And that's where all the taxidermied birds come in. He attaches their wings, feathers, and heads to something he calls *ornithopters*. They are not the long-lost cousins of velociraptors, but "small machines with mechanical wings that flap like those of birds and insects." He's tested pigeon, crow, and even hummingbird wings for their endurance and speed in hopes that his research "can create a revolution in the aviation industry"—though we can't help but worry that bird drones could also be used for surveillance, giving a sinister new meaning to the phrase "a bird's-eye view."

Montana

A freight train full of Coors Light and Blue Moon beer derailed just outside the aptly named town of Paradise, directly across from Quinn's Hot Springs Resort—and twenty-five rail cars carrying multiple cases of brew tumbled into the Clark Fork River. Talk about "bottoms up!"

Hungry Horse News reported that the incident "brought back memories" of a similar calamity some twenty years ago, when Montana Rail Link jumped the track between Paradise and Plains. Aside from liquid asphalt and corn syrup, the train was also carrying about 8,000 twelve-packs of Coors. Though the more recent derailment also involved a tank car carrying butane, a type of liquefied petroleum gas, it fortunately didn't cause any problems. Obviously, Bacchus and the other Beer Gods were smiling on Montana.

Idaho

Back in January, coyotes at the Schweitzer Mountain Ski Resort started "exhibiting highly unusual behavior" on the slopes, even chasing after skiers, according to *USA Today*. One woman was bitten, prompting Idaho Department of Fish and Game to warn the public that "patrons should be on guard and contact the agency if they spot coyotes," even if the coyotes claim to have legitimate ski passes. The usually shy nocturnal canines have even been seen prowling downtown Sandpoint in broad daylight, which the Department of Fish and Game said is "extremely rare activity." Asked for comment about what was up with the coyotes, a Road Runner spokesbird simply shrugged and said, "Beep-beep."

Washington

The *Walla Walla*, part of the Washington State Ferries fleet, experienced technical difficulties during its regular Saturday night route to Seattle from Bremerton. Fortunately, none of the 596 passengers got hurt and everyone (and, eventually, their cars) was safely offloaded. *Seattle Met* writer Haley Shapley and her cat, Kai, who were also aboard, published a timeline of events.

"4:20 to 4:22 p.m.: . . . lights on the ferry flicker. There's an ominous feeling in the air . . . A message crackles over the loudspeaker: 'We've lost steering and propulsion. Brace for impact.'"

"4:36 p.m.: We run aground."

"**4:37 p.m.**: I text: 'Okay we're okay. We crashed into the shore, but it was very soft.'"

Shapley described the fiasco with good humor. Life jackets were retrieved and donned. "Kids are crying, babies are screaming, and one guy is 100 percent sure he's still making it to the Mariners game tonight . . . There's a sea of orange and confusion."

"**5:10 p.m.**: We're asked to raise our hands and not lower them until we've been counted. There are almost 600 of us. My arm falls asleep three times before I'm counted." Not everyone cooperated, though:— Kai—adhering to the Cat Code of Conduct—refused to raise his paw.

Washington

Good news: Tokitae, also known as Lolita, the oldest killer whale in captivity, will return to her Salish Sea home waters after being held in Miami's Seaquarium since the early 1970s, when she was taken from her pod. KIRO7 contacted the Lummi Nation for a statement: "(Tok'tae) has a strong relationship with our homeland and all the natural resources therein. We are happy to hear that our relative, Sk'aliCh'elh'tenaut (Toki'tae), will have the opportunity to return home. She represents the story of all Native peoples that have experienced genocide and the bad policies that have been put in place to 'kill the Indian and save the man.' But more importantly, she represents our resilience and strength and our need for healing."

46

Baby Bears, White Whales, and "Freaky-Looking Fanged Fish," July 2023

Washington

If you live in the forest, eventually you're bound to run across forest critters—deer, flying squirrels, maybe Sasquatch—so when northwestern author Jonathan Evison encountered a bear cub on a trail near his cabin on Bainbridge Island, he was prepared. The *Kitsap Sun* reported Evison had been tromping in the woods near his cabin, in the Olympic foothills of Clallam County, when he heard a curious sound: A crying baby? Or a kitten maybe? He investigated and found a tiny bear cub at the base of a tree, scared and miserable. Evison, not wanting to interfere and hoping the mama bear would return, stepped quietly away. But the following day he returned and found the cub still crying, tangled up in branches underneath a tree. "It really wasn't much of a decision, and I just pretty much instinctively went up after it and freed it and then just put it back on its feet," he said. The cub latched onto Evison's ankle and began following him. Evison suspected that the mother had been killed by poachers; in any case, she clearly hadn't returned. So he contacted Fish and Wildlife and took the cub to West Sound Wildlife Shelter for medical attention. Then it was transferred to PAWS in Lynwood, a facility specifically created to assist lost or abandoned black bear cubs. There, the cub will hang out with his peers and learn how to be a bear. Eventually, it will be reintroduced to the wild. Evison said he felt he made the right choice when he rescued it: "What, am I supposed to kick it in the bushes and outrun it? I feel OK about it." But, he added, "We sure do miss him. He was such a cute little son of a gun."

California

Well, call me Ishmael! Apparently, white whales aren't confined to classic literature. *SFGate* reports Harbor Breeze Cruises, a whale-watching tour company, was returning from Catalina Island when Captain Kevin Nguyen spied the stream of mist that marks a spouting whale. An extremely rare "ghostly" white orca known as Frosty appeared with a pod of six other whales. It was a banner day, and not just for the schoolkids on Nguyen's boat. Within an hour, three other tour boats raced out with passengers eager to glimpse the legendary whale.

Oregon

It sounds like the opening scenes from a classic 1950s monster movie: "Freaky-looking fanged fishes found on Oregon beaches." These "freaky fish," which are known as lancetfish, are "scaleless with fanged jaws and huge eyes," "slinky bodies," and a "sail-like fin," according to the Associated Press. They're considered inedible (not that we can imagine anyone having the gumption to try) due to their "gelatinous flesh." The lancetfish, which normally live in tropical waters and travel as far north as the Bering Sea, washed ashore along 200 miles of coastline, an unusual occurrence, considering they dwell a mile beneath the ocean. Cue the bespectacled scientists scratching their heads while spooky organ music plays and the hero declares, "Bullets won't stop 'em," even as he springs into action to save his sweetheart, one of those dauntless "girl reporters" of yore.

Washington

A popular roadway was closed for several days due to a frightful pothole that wreaked havoc on motorist's' tires. The 5-by-4-foot pothole materialized on the on-ramp to northbound State Route 99. Video taken by

KIRO 7 shows the hole from below with bright blue sky visible through the West Seattle Bridge. The hole might not be a sinister portal to another dimension, but local motorists are certainly not pleased. The State Department of Transportation found no issues in August 2022, when it last inspected the road. But WSDOT did note that the road is over sixty years old—which is prehistoric in dog, or highway, years.

Colorado

The best part of waking up is not Folgers in your cup but . . . a cougar breakfasting on your front porch? Yikes! When Charles Zelenka was roused at 2:00 a.m. by an unholy racket, he assumed it was bears trying to break into his bear-proof dumpster, *Outdoor Life* reported. But when he investigated, he found a large elk in death throes: "I was just about ready to turn and go out the door, and a mountain lion popped up," Zelenka said. "So I grabbed my phone—I'm in my skivvies, I've just gotten out of bed—and start recording." Where's David Attenborough when you need him?

47

Orcas, Insects, and Other Roadside Attractions, August 2023

California

Orcas are in the news these days, with some attacking yachts off the coast of Spain. But orcas on North America's West Coast have also been busy, with one pod bringing bucket-list-brand delight to whale watchers in the Pacific. The lucky folks aboard a Monterey Bay Whale Watch tour encountered thirty orcas who were apparently working off the calories following a lavish sea lion buffet. "It was pure energy and celebration," Morgan Quimby of Monterey Bay Whale Watch told KTVU. Drone footage showed whales leaping into the air, spraying water from their blowholes, and playfully high-fiving the sea with their tails. And *SFGate* reported another large gathering—twenty-four orcas, spotted by the Oceanic Society near the Farallon Islands. So far, anyhow, California's orcas, unlike their Atlantic cousins, don't appear to be organizing any boat-bashing badassery. Responses to the Atlantic orcas' shenanigans are circulating on social media, with many observers cheering them on. As @DrBlackDeer posted: "The excitement y'all feel about the whales here lately is the same excitement we feel as Natives when buffalo start tossing tourists, like welcome to the Land Back movement."

Wyoming

Large groups of whales are wonderfully photogenic; gigantic hordes of crickets, now, are something else entirely. *Cowboy State Daily* reports that the "creepy" critters are giving folks the "heebie-jeebies" in Edgerton,

Wyoming, which has been invaded by them. The crickety confab is being compared to "something out of a horror movie—or the Bible." The crickets (*Anabrus simplex*; also called Mormon crickets though, as far as we know, they're lapsed) are swarming Edgerton's streets, highway, and homes by the thousands—no, by the *millions*—and creating some serious problems. Driving gets dodgy because the squishy bug guts make roads super-slick. "It's like driving on ice," said Travis Anderson, who works for the town of Edgerton. The crickets have also invaded Elko, Nevada, KUTV reported. Elko resident Colette Reynolds summed it up: "It's bugging me, it's really bugging me." The crickets are cannibalistic and greedily gobble each other, dead or alive. But other than that—and the traffic hazards, and the smelly decaying carcasses everywhere— they're basically harmless.

California

Fox5SanDiego.com reported that a popular San Diego DJ, Randy "R Dub!" Williams, has founded his own micronation, the "Republic of Slowjamastan," on 11.07 acres of desert in Imperial County, about 100 miles from San Diego. As "Sultan" and "Supreme Leader," Williams runs everything: crocs (the footwear, not the reptiles) are prohibited, and biting into string cheese, "mumble rap" music, and driving in the left passing lane, unless you're actually passing, are all forbidden. Williams has big plans for Slowjamastan, including an armadillo farm and an all-you-can-eat Mongolian BBQ restaurant. But no crickets—yet.

Wyoming

Here's another story from the *Cowboy State Daily*. Roadside attractions make road trips memorable, adding a dash of whimsy to the vacay photos, whether it's Boise's Big Idaho Potato Hotel or the World's Largest Pistachio® in Alamogordo, New Mexico. Such attractions are as iconic as the Grand Tetons or Devils Tower, although some critics consider them aesthetically offensive. Take the Big Boy hamburger statue outside of Wapiti, near Yellowstone National Park's East Entrance. The Wapiti Big Boy appears out of his element, albeit cheerfully so. But what on earth is he doing here? The statue's owner, James Geier, said: "I heard people say it just showed up, like Easter Island, and nobody knows how it got there." But Geier knows Big Boy's true origin because he's the one who installed it, in 2013, and now maintains it for all to see. The cute little guy—rescued from an authentic California Big Boy restaurant—seems harmless enough; he lacks that Ronald McDonald "scary clown" vibe.

Washington

If twenty-four-hour polka music and all-you-can-eat wiener schnitzel isn't enough to thrill you, hold on to your lederhosen, because Leavenworth, a quaint Bavarian-themed town in the North Cascades, has added a roller coaster. The Leavenworth Adventure Park's new Tumwater Twister Alpine Coaster boasts a 2,700-foot track and a vertical drop of 234 feet, and cruises up to 27 mph, the *Wenatchee World* reported. Diana Thronsen, seventy-five, was one of the first to try it: "It's really fun and really scary with terrific views of Wenatchee River and the whole valley. When I wasn't screaming, it was beautiful." Which sounds to us like the perfect motto for this column.

48

Bathroom Bison, Foul-Smelling Flowers, and Outlaw Otters on the Lam, September 2023

Wyoming

It's one thing to get stuck between a rock and a hard place, but between a bathroom and a 2,000-pound bison? Now, that's a hairy situation. A visitor was trying to leave the restroom at Yellowstone National Park when he realized that a huge bison was blocking the way, *Cowboy State Daily* reported. Unlike the other tourists we cover in this column, though, he reacted intelligently, waiting inside the bathroom until the coast was clear and periodically peeking out to check. Taylor Caropolo posted a video of the "awkward encounter" to the Facebook group "Yellowstone: Invasion of the Idiots." This time, however, the bison was the invader, and the human, for a change, behaved responsibly.

California

If you thought the orca attacks off the coasts of Spain, Portugal, and Scotland were surprising, this news will otterly amaze you. "Otter 841," a five-year-old female, has been harassing locals in Santa Cruz, NPR reports, and even stealing surfboards. The otter's unusual behavior has wildlife officials officially baffled, although the California Department of Fish and Wildlife believes that 841, who was raised by humans at the Monterey Bay Aquarium, simply never developed a healthy wariness of people. While this might explain 841's lack of fear, it does not explain why she's turned to crime. Normally, we think of otters as cuddly and adorable, not as schoolyard bullies or the perps in a game of *Grand Theft Surfboard*. Wildlife officials have been trying to capture the "outlaw" otter and rehome her in the interest of public safety, as well as her own, but 841 has thus far evaded them. Meanwhile, she's gained a considerable fan following on Instagram. Several online petitions advocating for her freedom are circulating—one has over 50,000 signatures—and an Instagram page, @thesurfingotter, overflows with memes and parody images. One of them compares 841 to Batman from the 2008 film *The Dark Knight*, solemnly declaring: "She's the hero Santa Cruz deserves, but not the one it needs right now. So we'll hunt her. Because she can take it. Because she's not our hero. She's a silent guardian, a watchful protector. A dark knight." Whether 841 is actually the superhero we need right now remains to be seen. But we must admit she looks pretty badass decked out in the Dark Knight's mask.

California/Washington

There's no doubt that, as NPR reports, the legendary corpse flower is the "rockstar of the plant world." And we're in luck, because right now there are three—count 'em, THREE—blooming in California and Washington this summer. Horticulturalists are thrilled, because this very rare and elusive plant can go seven to ten years between blooms. These particular otherworldly looking plants can be found at San Francisco's Conservatory of Flowers, the San Diego Botanic Gardens, and the Amazon Spheres in Seattle. If you plan to visit—and ya better hustle, because the blossoming stage lasts only 24–48 hours—be sure to bring nose plugs. This hardcore Goth cousin of the calla lily—its scientific name is *Amorphophallus titanium*, or the titan arum—is impossible to miss. The blossom can grow up to 8 feet tall and emits a distinctive fragrance, much like rotting meat. Ari Novy, president and CEO of the San Diego Botanic Garden, said it smells as if you put "your teenager's dirty laundry in a big black garbage bag" with "some hamburger meat, maybe some fish, a little garlic and some parmesan cheese. And you left that by the side of the road on a very hot desert day for about 24 hours." Sounds, um, delightful—perfect for Valentine's Day.

Washington/Oregon

If you're hiking along a trail in the woods and encounter a gigantic Nordic troll that seems to have wandered out of *The Lord of the Rings*, no need to pinch yourself, you're not dreaming. Plans are underway to install six of the whimsical sculptures within natural landscapes across the Pacific Northwest. The trolls, which range from 12 to 20 feet in height, are created by Danish artist and environmentalist Thomas Dambo and constructed with the help of volunteers (human, not elvish), using recycled materials. Dambo has built a hundred troll sculptures around the globe, though these will be the first in the Pacific Northwest, *Geek Wire* reports. The sculptures are meant to "tell a tale of protecting nature and honoring the land and waterways." Nice to know that not all trolls are on social media.

49

Backscratching Bears, Seismic Singers, and Happy Birthday to Herman the Sturgeon, October 2023

What's a homeowner supposed to do when a grizzly bear takes a shine to their 6-foot-tall shed and starts using it as a combination scent post/back scratcher/claw-sharpening-and-nail-polishing device? Jamie Goguen realized she had a *beary* big problem indeed when a very large grizzly—estimated at between 700 and 800 pounds—began enthusiastically tearing up the generator shed on her property. Fortunately, the folks at Montana Fish, Wildlife and Parks know a thing or two about bruins, and they came up with a fur-raising solution to the problem, *Field & Stream* reported, teaming up with Goguen to install electric fencing that should discourage future visits and "prevent further conflicts with humans and structures." We just hope the grizzly finds a decent replacement. You know how it is when you get an itch; you've just got to scratch it, no matter where you are.

Washington

Taylor Swift's "Eras Tour" is not just breaking records; it's keeping local seismologists busy. The *Seattle Times* reported that all the singing, dancing, and screaming generated seismic activity comparable to a 2.3 magnitude earthquake during Swift's back-to-back, sold-out shows at Seattle's Lumen Field in July. A reported 72,171 fans were rocking out, and that's a lot of Swifties. Scientists have been warning us that "The Big One" is due to hit the Pacific Northwest any day now. We just hadn't realized they were talking about a pop star.

Montana

When the newspaper's front page features an above-the-fold story about an "unidentified electric vehicle" siphoning power from the local electric utility, chances are it's either a slow news day or a very small town. The vehicle in question, a Tesla Model Y, belonged to Chad Lauterbach, who drove from LA—with his girlfriend, Allis Markham, a well-known taxidermist—to Ekalaka to volunteer at the county museum's annual dinosaur festival, the *Montana Free Press* reported. Unfortunately, Ekalaka, population 400, is located in a vehicle-charging wasteland two hours from the nearest Walmart. The car's navigation system began "throwing out warnings" during the long drive, but if worse came to worst, Lauterbach hoped that a good Samaritan would rescue them—though it might take days to recharge a vehicle using a 120-volt outlet tucked away in someone's garage. However, they got lucky; there was an unlocked outlet connected to a utility pole on Ekalaka's main street. Markham hesitated to use it, but Lauterbach said that if anyone noticed his car and got worried, they could get in touch with the museum director, whom he'd previously notified. Surprise, someone did notice it. The next day, Lauterback's Tesla appeared on the *Ekalaka Eagle*'s front page, described as a "UEV: Unidentified electric vehicle," and the article questioned whether the car's owner had actually paid for what it dubbed the "stolen volts." Marham hurried over to the power company, the Southeast Electric Cooperative, and told the front desk that she was "here to pay for the crimes of the UEV," causing the staff to howl with laughter. The couple ended up paying $60 for the electricity, enough to cover the band that used the outlet during the dinosaur festival's street dance. Asked about whether the utility co-op has plans to install an electric charging station, manager Tye Williams replied that they'd been "kicking around the idea," but Ekalaka is so remote it isn't on the state's priority list. Williams agreed that they'd need to do something within the next decade, "or some amount of time." Markham, who had warned Lauterbach about charging his car without permission, clearly got a charge out of the whole situation: "Having an 'I told you so' on the front page of the paper is very validating for a woman," she quipped.

Oregon

"Happy birthday" to Herman the Sturgeon, a renowned 10-foot-long, over 500-pound fish who recently turned eighty-eight, KGW8 News reports. The stately birthday dame—this particular Herman is actually female, not male—resides at the Bonneville Dam Fish Hatchery, a popular site for folks to visit and learn about fish hatcheries, conservation, and really big fish like Herman. "It's the perfect place to have an interpretative center for sturgeons and talk about conservation of the species and then just enjoy a really wonderful day on grounds that are beautifully manicured and landscaped," said Tim Greseth, executive director of the Oregon Wildlife Foundation. Fun fact: Sturgeons have been around since Jurassic times, though, as we all know, a lady—even if she's a fish named Herman—seldom reveals her true age.

50

Too Many Snakes, a Hard-Rockin' Dog, and a GPS Truck-Up, November 2023

Colorado

Here's an unfortunate example of AI giving someone a real bum steer. A tractor-trailer's navigational guidance system "trucked up" in a major way, inconveniencing slews of sightseers and campers en route to the picturesque Crystal Mill, six miles east of Marble in Gunnison County. Just how big a mistake did the GPS make? Well, it sent the driver up the very steep, very narrow, and very rocky Daniels Hill—a road navigable only by four-wheel-drive vehicles, jeeps, dirt bikes, hikers, and people who scare the bejeezus out of viewers on *IRT: Deadliest Roads*. The misguidance left the big rig jackknifed across the road for forty hours until three tow trucks could remove it. Samantha Smith Wilkey, owner of Crystal River Jeep Tours, said she lost ten bookings while the road was blocked, but she doesn't blame the driver. "The driver went above and beyond," she told *Aspen Daily News*. "It's not the trucking company. It's the GPS software company." Smith Wilkey added that misguided guidance systems are misguiding drivers to remote forestry roads rather than correct routes to Gunnison or even Denver, concluding: "There is a glitch in this area." Yes—and apparently a glitch in the matrix.

California

Every dog has its day, they say, but most canines don't spend theirs howling it up at a free Metallica concert. An unusually resourceful metal fan—and German shepherd—named Storm snuck out of her Inglewood home and somehow slipped unnoticed through the gate and past security to settle comfortably into a seat of her own at SoFi Stadium, KTLA 5 reported. Storm's owners were baffled when a photo of their pooch hanging out with concertgoers ended up on social media, but they were happy to welcome her home after she spent the night at an animal shelter.

California

Maybe it's something in the dog food, because another unusual canine incident occurred in San Juan Bautista. KSBW.com reported that a sure-paw'd terrier "learned a new meaning to the word 'bark' when it got stuck in a tree." The dog somehow climbed 20 feet up a tree and got marooned out on a limb. The Hollister Fire Department rescued the pooch by deploying a safety net, climbing the tree, and carrying the pup down. Maybe there was another metal band playing nearby, and the dog just wanted a good view?

Arizona

An understandably shaken Mesa homeowner contacted a snake-wrangling outfit after discovering a tangle of rattlesnakes lounging around in his garage, Fox10 Phoenix reported. The homeowner originally *guessss*-timated that there were three, but there were actually twenty: five adult western diamondbacks and fifteen babies. Oh, and one of the snakes was pregnant with babies—or eggs, technically. Like certain members of Congress, rattlesnakes are ovoviviparous, meaning that their eggs hatch inside the mama-rattler, who then gives birth to live young. Snake-wrangler Marissa Maki, who found the reptiles nestled cozily around the hot water heater, used specialized tongs to grab them and carefully place them in plastic buckets for their relocation journey to the desert. Rattlesnake Solutions' owner Bryan Hughes said proudly, "This is our record for the most rattlesnakes caught in one call!" Given the number of shed snakeskins they found, as many as forty may have resided there at some point. As Maki observed, in what we consider a definite understatement, "That is a lot of snakes."

Oregon

Here's a great example of positive messaging. Bella Organic Farm on Sauvie Island is using the 2.7 miles of pathways of its seven-acre corn maze to say something important: "No more silence. End gun violence." The words are accompanied by a peace sign and heart shapes. A Bella Organic spokesperson told *The Oregonian*, "We hope this year's maze will bring our community together." That seems like a message no one could get lost in.

Washington

Horse racing is traditionally the Sport of Kings, but Auburn's Emerald Downs Race Course has something for commoners too. About twenty seniors hit the track at the inaugural "Grandparents Race" held during Grandparents Weekend, King5 reported. Steve Butler from Everett, who took home the prize, told Emerald Downs that the last time he'd raced was against a lineman during a high school football game fifty years earlier. The popular racetrack hosts races for horses as well as for corgis and bulldogs, not to mention the T-Rex World Championship, which we were slightly disappointed to learn involves people wearing costumes rather than contestants running shrieking from live dinosaurs.

51

Sagebrush Sasquatch, Irritable Elk, and Spiders That Aren't from Mars, December 2023

Colorado

Here's a hair-raising encounter from the Centennial State, reported by the *Denver Post*. Shannon and Stetson Parker were enjoying a relaxing jaunt through the San Juan Mountains on the Durango and Silverton Narrow Gauge Railroad when Stetson spotted something unusual. "We were looking for elk in the mountains and my husband sees something moving and then can't really explain it. So he's like, 'Bigfoot!'" Shannon told the *New York Post*. "It was at least six, seven feet or taller. It matched the sage in the mountains so much that he's like camouflaged when crouching down." Shannon reported the sighting on her Facebook page, noting that the man sitting next to them on the train also grabbed his phone and started recording whatever it was they'd spotted. Shannon posted his footage and her own photos on her Facebook page. "Y'all, out of the hundreds of people on the train, three or four of us actually saw, as Stetson says in the video, the ever-elusive creature Bigfoot," Shannon wrote. "I don't know about y'all, but we believe."

However, some Bigfoot experts, including Jim Myers, owner of the Sasquatch Outpost in Bailey, Colorado, and paranormal researcher Alan Megargle, weren't convinced. *Westword* reported that Myers regards the sighting as a hoax, and Megargle diagnosed it as a case of "Squatch Fever." Myers and Megargle collaborated on the documentary *The Bigfoot of Bailey Colorado and Its Portal*, which explains why the elusive cryptid is so darn elusive: "Apparently, it's inter-dimensional and can travel between worlds through an alien portal located in a Native American sacred tree." *Okaaay*. As one of the T-shirts Myers sells reminds us: "Bigfoot doesn't believe in you either."

Utah

If you are a fan of legendary environmental activist Edward Abbey, author of *The Monkey Wrench Gang* and *Desert Solitaire,* then you'd better sit down for this next story. The *Durango Telegraph* reported that a Moab housing development company broke ground for, well, for an Edward Abbey–themed subdivision featuring streets named after the author's work, even though new development and road building are utterly antithetical to everything that the curmudgeonly Abbey stood for. Lifelong friends of Abbey said that dedicating a subdivision to his memory goes against his legacy, to put it mildly. The subdivision, which will be dubbed "The Abbey," is expected to include eighty houses on approximately 22 acres within the Moab city limits. Street names include "Monkey Wrench Way," named after Abbey's novel about anti-development eco-saboteurs, as well as "Hayduke Court," named after the guy in the book who plants explosives at Glen Canyon Dam.

If you're wondering, as we were, *WTF were the developers thinking?* Mike Bynum, a Moab businessman, explained that The Abbey was years in the making and is intended as a homage to the writer. After all, *Desert Solitaire* was set in nearby Arches National Park and helped put Moab on the map. But did the developers actually *read* any of Abbey's books? Next on the drawing board: "Silent Spring Pesticides Inc." and "Black Beauty's Olde Horsemeat Shoppe."

Washington

Since 2012 Whidbey Island has hosted a lone elk known as Bruiser, treating him as a welcome guest. Ralph Downes, an officer for the Washington Department of Fish and Wildlife, has been Bruiser's "de facto guardian angel" since the elk first appeared on the island, the *Seattle Times* reported. But since October, there have been warnings to watch out around Bruiser. KOMO News reported that the elk can get ornery and has been picking fights with cars. "This time of year, he tends to get a little frustrated. He doesn't have anyone to wrestle with and he can't find anyone to have as a companion," Downes said. It's happened before: in 2017 he—Bruiser, not Downes—was tranquilized after getting ensnarled with a buoy and 30 feet of mooring line. Maybe the buoy was tailgating?

California

Ziggy Stardust appears to have lost a few spiders on his way back to Mars. Either that, or maybe it's just nature. According to KION46, residents across California's Central Coast reported "a sticky web-like substance" falling from the sky. But don't panic: John E. Banks, a professor at California State University Monterey Bay, thinks the substance derives from "ballooning," a method that spiders use to get from one place to another. "It's a special term we use for how spiders disperse from habitat to habitat," Banks said. They spin out spider silk and use it like a parachute— just as efficient as human air travel, and no carbon emissions involved.

52

Beautiful Bats, Big Boulders, and a Seven-Armed Octopus, January 2024

Oregon

William ShakespEAR, a female Townsend's big-eared bat from Butte Falls, Oregon, defended her title for the second year in a row in the "Bat Beauty Contest," an annual contest hosted by the Bureau of Land Management to raise awareness about bat conservation, OPD News reported. Townsend's big-eared bats are noted for having, well, very big ears—ears that measure half the length of their bodies. The contest, which coincides with International Bat Week, accepts photos of bats taken on public lands across the country starting October 24 and ending on Halloween. Emma Busk, a BLM wildlife technician, photographed the winner. "There are a lot of myths around bats, but they're amazing wildlife and they contribute so much to our ecosystem," Busk told OPD. Not only do they keep the mosquito populations down, some look absolutely fabulous in the itsy-bitsy-teeny-weeny bikini competition.

Arizona

Congratulations to Alfredo Aliaga, ninety-two, who became the oldest person to complete the Grand Canyon's rim-to-rim hike, 24 miles long and with an elevation gain and loss of over 10,000 feet, *Backpacker* reported. Aliaga made it in twenty-one hours over two days, breaking a Guinness world record for being the oldest person to finish (verification pending), succeeding former record holder John Jempka, age ninety-one and 152 days old. This wasn't Aliaga's first rodeo: a Spanish-born geology enthusiast, he's hiked the rim-to-rim twice, first in 2019, with his daughter and son-in-law, and again last year. Aliaga's wife died in 2006, his son-in-law, Jurgen Buchenau, told *Backpacker*, and he comforted himself by revisiting places they'd loved, including the Grand Canyon. Aliaga—who trained by walking three hours a day in Berlin, Germany, where he lives—is already planning a fourth hike in 2024. Meanwhile, we're exhausted just thinking about all those back-and-forth transatlantic airline flights.

Oregon

If you're going to Bend, Oregon, keep an eye out for Big Obvious Boulder, a.k.a.: "Bob," a rock with almost 6,000 Facebook fans. Bob is renowned for what you might call its "magnetic personality": it tends to attract careless or distracted motorists, whose cars somehow end up high-centered on top of it, *Central Oregon Daily News* reported. The boulder sits at the entrance of a plaza at the corner of NE Third Street and Franklin Avenue, in case you want to drive over—carefully, please—and take a selfie, as scores of fans have. Kristin Morris, director of hearing care for My Hearing Centers, said that trucks seem to find Bob irresistible. "Trucks have hit it mostly and dragged the rock into the middle of the parking lot, and it's had to be replaced back into its position many times," Morris said. "People have actually driven on top of the rock and their cars get stuck." According to Morris, this happened six times in just the last month. The people in those cars probably think "Obvious" is the wrong name for the boulder. Then again, Bob appears to be, literally, impossible to miss, at least for some drivers.

Washington

A strange looking many-tentacled creature that washed up on a Whidbey Island beach has had scientists at odds about its identity, KentReporter.com reported. Ron Newberry of Admirals Cove found the sea creature on Ebey's Landing beach one morning at low tide and sent a photo to the *Whidbey News-Times*. "I didn't know for sure it was an octopus," Newberry wrote in an email. "It's pretty common to see large jelly-fish washed up on shore." When he posted the photo on the Whidbey Camano Land Trust social media pages, it attracted a lot of notice. An engineer from the Seattle Aquarium thought it looked like "a Dumbo octopus from the deep sea," while a University of Washington biology professor could not identify it and sent the photo to other biologists for their opinion. Soon scientists from across the country were weighing in, including researchers from the Monterey Bay Aquarium Research Institute, the National Oceanic and Atmospheric Administration, and the Smithsonian Institution. After much fanfare, a consensus was reached, confirming that the curious creature was a *Haliphron atlanticus*: a seven-armed octopus. The name is actually a misnomer: males really do have an eighth arm, but it's kept "tucked up inside in a sac near its eye" and used for breeding, don't ask us how. Anyway, hats—or gloves—off to Haliphron: we generally expect octopuses to have eight appendages, but here in the USA, you have the right to bear as many arms as you want.

3 Bonus Slices and Outtakes with Extra Cheese

53

In the Good Way
Looking at Tribal Humor

1. The Indigenous Whoopee Cushion School of Comedy

Since time immemorial my Indigenous ancestors have practiced the sacred art of comedy. Comedy gold classics such as the whoopee cushion predate first contact. And chokecherry-cream-pies-in-the-face are actually paleolithic. Cave wall paintings provide the earliest clues to the existence of ancient Native American shtick. Whoopee cushions, sometimes called "toot pillows," were originally made from the bladders of deer or bison; the bladder was inflated and tied off, much like a modern-day balloon. Prehistoric examples of whoopee cushions along with shards of ancient pie pans were discovered at an archaeological dig near the famous Corn Palace in Mitchell, South Dakota. Evidence of coup sticks were also excavated, proving that slapstick (quite literally a "slap stick"), was a highly regarded cultural custom.

Except for the opening line, "Since time immemorial my Indigenous ancestors have practiced the sacred art of comedy," I'm obviously joking.

Suffice to say that, whatever direction my ancestors' humor may have taken, there have been very well-established conclusions about Native humor over the decades. A starting point is author, activist, and historian Vine Deloria Jr. (Standing Rock Sioux). His seminal essay "Indian Humor," from his book *Custer Died for Your Sins*, details specific jokes—from the "Indian jokes canon" as it were—and this essay is cited repeatedly in Native Studies scholarship. Deloria wrote: "One of the best ways to understand a people is to know what makes them laugh. Laughter encompasses the limits of the soul. In humor life is redefined and accepted. Irony and satire provide much keener insights into a group's collective psyche and values than do years of research."

After so many years one might wonder if his essay holds up; is it still relevant in 2023? Definitely so, particularly the Custer jokes he cites. Natives still enjoy a good Custer zinger, evidenced by how many memes and cartoons I see on my social media feeds—especially around June 25th, anniversary of the Battle of the Greasy Grass, or Battle of Little Bighorn. In fact, because of social media, Native satire is more accessible than ever. TikTok, Instagram, and Facebook are the new smoke signals, the new moccasin telegraph. Some of the humor would make church ladies clutch their pearls—or cause those straitlaced aunties to clutch their beads (an exception being Willie Jack's Auntie B, portrayed on *Reservation Dogs*, whose beadwork is rather, um, interesting). I imagine Deloria would LOL. Heartily. If one wonders why Indians might appreciate saucy humor, they need only look at creation stories and "folklore" of tribal peoples: our stories are full of sexual mishaps, risqué characters, and ribald humor. There are stories about tricksters lusting after various targets, stories of young women seducing star people, vagina dentata tales, and more.

2. Indian Humor Takes Its Gloves Off

In the aftermath of the Greasy Grass battlefield, was it humor, poetic justice, or both that prompted Cheyenne women to take up sewing needles and pierce the eardrums of the defeated General Custer? According to testimony this was so that he might hear better in the afterlife—certainly better than when he was alive. And was a similar concept or sensibility used following the Sioux Uprising? The Dakota had been denied food or credit by the white traders while being forbidden to hunt outside of reservation boundaries. The people were starving and a trader, Andrew Myrick, said they should eat grass. Myrick was slain during the uprising, and when his body was found, his mouth had been stuffed with grass. The Apsáalooke (Crow) artist Wendy Red Star refers to a story about Medicine Crow to describe "Indian humor." Or more specifically, Apsáalooke humor. Red Star recounts that Medicine Crow possessed a "weird and wicked sense of humor." When Medicine Crow and others killed some horse thieves, he cut off one of their hands, and he later used the horse thief's severed hand to shake hands with the reservation's Indian agent. Red Star said, "The fact that this one guy had this bizarre sense of humor—I want people to know that."

So when I run across content that's rugged or "cringe," while at the same time really funny, I remember that Indians have been practitioners of this brand of humor, morbid or gallows humor—*but in the good way*—for a very long time, *since time immemorial.* One example of this scathing humor occurred during Standing Rock: Native folks were posting memes and jokes on social media that responded to the water protectors on the front lines being viciously attacked by dogs. Memes and jokes that were posted less than twenty-four hours after protectors had *actually* been viciously attacked by dogs. Is this schadenfreude—deriving amusement or pleasure from witnessing others' misfortunes? Or does it fall into the category of transcending trauma through humor and teasing—another hallmark of Native humor? A more subtle and uplifting perspective on Native humor used during Standing Rock was Cannupa Hanska Luger's Mirror Shield Project: dozens of protectors held up mirrors that reflected back upon riot police at the front lines. Parody holds up a mirror to adversaries through nonviolent resistance. And in this instance, literally. While this frontline action would not necessarily be described as "humor," much like piercing Custer's eardrums following Greasy Grass or the irony of stuffing grass in Myrick's mouth, they are consistent with a particular sensibility, which strikes me as a sort of distant cousin to humor. At least in hindsight.

3. Satire as Decolonial Coup Stick or Settler Spanking

All too often the media and publishing industrial complex seem very invested in our tragedy and redemption narratives—a kind of poverty tourism for public consumption. Of course, it's fair to say that Western literature has always been about death and tragedy. Native

American literature easily finds its place within those themes: books, photojournalism, and films about intergenerational trauma. Stories about the plight of the Native Americans, our struggles, oppression, disappearances, and genocide. I often wonder about the opposite end of this continuum: intergenerational joy, creativity, and humor. But let's not leave out intergenerational sarcasm, intergenerational whimsy, or intergenerational weirdness! Can I even claim being Native if I don't have a personal trauma narrative replete with a strong message of hope and redemption?

This concept of "Indian humor" or "Indigenous joy," represented in art, especially as a binary or even antidote to "Indigenous trauma" or "poverty tourism" for consumption or exploitation, rings hollow and prescriptive to me. It is helpful to consider humor and joy as being fundamental values encompassing the human experience while also considering there are definitive features, content, and attitudes characterizing "Native humor." "Native Humor" is a very comprehensive discourse, and I wonder about de-labeling it, perhaps inviting the idea that Indians are human (a bold thing to state, I know!) Can we conceive humor as human? Does "Native humor" require its label because we are not considered fully human?

Never mind—*smashes huckleberry cream pie in face.*

4. My Two Cents

When I wrote an article on Wendy Red Star's work for the *New Yorker*, during the editing phase I was asked to elaborate on the concept of "Indi'n humor," particularly because Red Star's work is quite often satiric. I was thrilled to throw in my two cents, especially for such a prominent publication. Rarely are Natives asked to contribute to such conversations, let alone discuss something as niche (at least to the mainstream) as Native humor. (Although that's certainly changing.) I submitted my "two cents":

While "Indi'n humor" may contrast from American humor in a lot of ways, perhaps its most prevalent characteristic is how often it solicits explanation. And how self-referential it is, to the point that whenever a Native makes a joke, those who are listening respond by appreciatively acknowledging their use of "Indian humor." After centuries of being mischaracterized as stoic and austere, it is plausible, even necessary to self-reference our use of humor as a means to reassert our humanity. And of course, this in itself is an example of Indi'n humor. Without shared context or insider knowledge of history, or lived experience, certain ironies and particularly gallows-brand humor—another tell-tale signature—can't be fully appreciated beyond the surface.

Not surprisingly, the paragraph was cut. Too tangential and off topic, I would guess. I'm not sure "Indi'n humor" can be described in less than fifty words, can it? The editors might've thought I was being cheeky in my response—"how often it solicits explanation. And how self-referential it is . . ." Except that this is very true! I hear so often that Native humor was our means of survival; that Native humor is an example of our resiliency; that Native humor is medicine, laughter is healing, which are all accurate features of our cultures, but what I had been trying to describe was that when a joke is made, in whatever setting, all too often it's bookended with these truisms. And while these are certainly uplifting, at times I'm impatient with their predictability. I think our humor is more complex than that. A lot more complex than I have room to explore in just this one essay, considering there's more than enough about Indian humor to fill an entire book.

5. Indians Appearing in TV Situational Comedies and Rom Coms . . . Wait, What?!

With the emergence of Indigenous comedians and showrunners finally given a platform within Hollywood entertainment and television sitcoms, hilarious shows like *Reservation Dogs* and *Rutherford Falls* are finally offering a perspective not often viewed on the national stage. Indigenous humor, or "Indi'n humor," is nothing new, of course—but its reach has expanded. It's gone from "grass (dance) roots," so to speak, to mainstream. And while this development certainly has its benefits, optimizing awareness and visibility of Indigenous issues, obviously, it also sends a strong message that we still exist. We've always been here, wise-cracking and laughing with our grandmas and grandpas, aunties and cousins around the kitchen table, meeting up at powwows, graduation picnics, and well, yes, funerals. We've always found that circle to join in where we joke, tease, stretch the truth, and entertain. And I'm left to wonder: why has it taken America so long to figure out that Indi'n humor is worth the production value, worth the trouble of investing capital into? To create "content" for television? And not just television series but also theater productions, stand-up comedy, and films. It's especially gratifying to see the shift from non-Natives writing *about* Indigenous people, to Indigenous-created stories and sitcoms written *by* Indigenous people. The shift is dramatic—the white colonialist gaze being supplanted by an obviously more accurate and dynamic perspective is worthy of celebration. And in that development, Indigenous creators are being directly compensated, also. There's no denying that Indians participate in capitalism as much as the rest of the world. So, receiving story credit and financial gains from telling our own stories represents significant progress. It benefits our young people to see themselves represented in media. Not as wooden stereotypes, butts of jokes, or mockeries, but as fully developed and complex human beings.

6. Let Me Just Leave You with This

Since time immemorial my Indigenous ancestors have practiced the sacred art of comedy. It is not widely known that legendary Hunkpapa leader Sitting Bull was a notorious practical joker. He often pranked Red Cloud during tribal council by placing a whoopee cushion beneath Red Cloud's buffalo robe with hilarious results! But he stole all his best material from the band's heyoka, Pretty Wallowing Woman, and passed it off as his own. In fact, it was Ernest Iron Necklace, a great-great-grandson of Pretty Wallowing Woman, who originated the Take-My-Wife-Please shtick that was made famous by comedian Henny Youngman. In a 1967 *Newsweek* article, the famous "King of the One-Liners" credits Iron Necklace as his inspiration for comedy. "Iron Necklace was my comedy spirit patronus," Youngman said.

54

Beets

In fourth-grade history class, I learned that the Plains Indians weren't cut out to be farmers. The government tried to get them to plant corn and stuff, but it was a no-win situation. No matter how hard the Indians fought against progress, manifest destiny, and the American Dream, they'd never win. This history lesson occurred around the same time the U.S. media began its hyper-ecological awareness campaigns. All kinds of theories were developed that said the earth was heading toward another ice age—whereas today scientists tell us the earth is getting hotter. It was during this time that my father's beliefs about the demise of the twentieth century began tipping toward fanaticism. The *Whole Earth Catalog* took up residence in our home, and he began reciting from it as if it were scripture. He wanted us all to get back to nature. I think he would have sold the house and moved us into the mountains to raise goats and chickens, but my mother—who regularly didn't have much of a say in family decisions—must have threatened to leave him for good if he took his plans to fruition.

So, he settled for gardening.

Actually, gardening is too light a word for the blueprints he drew up, which would transform our medium-sized backyard into a small farming community.

One day I returned home from school and discovered my father shoveling manure from a pile tall as a two-story building. I couldn't help but wonder where he'd ever purchased such a magnificent pile of shit. Impressive though it was, I doubt the neighbors shared his enthusiasm, and I wouldn't have been surprised if they had been circulating a petition to have it removed.

"Good, you're home! Grab a rake."

Knowing I didn't stand a chance arguing, I did just as he ordered, and I spent the rest of the day raking manure, thinking the Plains Indians opted not to farm because they knew enough not to. I think my father would have kept us out there shoveling and raking until after midnight if my mother hadn't insisted I come in the house and do my homework. The next day I had blisters on my hands and couldn't hold a pencil.

"Hard work builds character," my father preached. "Children have it too easy today, all you want to do is sit around and pick lint out of your belly buttons."

I was saved from hard labor the remainder of the week because during music class the blisters on my hands spontaneously burst open, fountaining blood all over the song sheets like stigmata. Poor Mrs. O'Reilly gasped and rapidly began genuflecting before pulling herself together and sending me home. She never did look me straight in the face after that.

"No pain, no gain," Father said. "Next time, wear the gloves."

The following weekend our suburban nuclear unit had transformed into the spitting image of the Sunshine Family Dolls. I began calling my sister Dewdrop, myself Starshine. I renamed my mother Corn Woman and my father Reverend Buck. Reverend Buck considered it his personal mission in life to convert us from our heathen, Hungry Man TV dinner, Bisquick and Pop-Tart existence.

"Do you realize that with all these preservatives, after you're dead and buried your body will take several extra years to completely decompose?" Father said.

This wasn't exactly a concern ranking high on my list, being that I was *only* nine, but my sister Judy summed it up with, "I don't care, I plan on being cremated."

As the "good reverend's" wife and children, we must have represented some deprived tribe of soulless, bereft Indians, and he designated himself to take us—the godless parish—under his wing.

Mother resigned herself to his plans, and we reluctantly followed her example. When she was growing up on the reservation, her family cultivated and planted every season, so gardening wasn't some incomprehensibly exotic activity like walking on stilts or running across hot coals. The difference, I guess, was that her family planted only what they could use. They were conservative. But my father's plans resembled a large midwestern crop, minus the tractors. He even drew up sketches of an irrigation system he borrowed from the *Whole Earth Catalog*.

It was a nice dream. His heart was in the right place. I'm sure the U.S. government, back in the days of treaties, relocation, and designation of reservation lands, thought their intentions were noble too. I kind of admired my father for his big ideas but sided with my mother on this one.

My father was always more interested in the idea of something rather than the actuality; to him bigger meant better. My father liked large things—generous mass, quantity, weight. For him they represented progress, ambition, trust. Try as he might to be some kind of renegade, adopt Indian beliefs and philosophies, and even go so far as to marry an Indian woman, he still could never avoid the obvious truth: he was a white man. He liked to build large things.

"What are you planning to do with all these vegetables?" my mother asked.

"Freeze and can them, of course," Father said. My mother was about to say something else but then looked as if she thought the better of it. I knew what she was thinking though. She was thinking Father expected *her* to freeze and can them. And she didn't look thrilled at the prospect of being pressed into service.

My father may have accused her of being an *apple* (red on the outside, white on the inside) from time to time, even went so far as to refer to her as *apple pie*—what he considered a term of endearment—but Mother must have retained much of that Plains Indian stoic refusal to derive pleasure from farming large acreage.

Father assigned each of us a row. Mother was busily stooped over, issuing corn into the soil as if offering gems of sacrifice to the earth goddess. I was in charge of the radishes and turnips, which up until that day I'd known only through tales of Peter Rabbit stealing from Mr. McGregor's garden. I bent down over my chore, all the while on keen lookout for small white rabbits accessorized in gabardine trousers.

My sister was diligently poking holes into the soil for her onions when our collie began nosing around the corn rows scouting for a place to pee. "Get out of the corn, Charlie!" I yelled.

Father chuckled and said, "Hey, a scorned corndog."

Mother rolled her eyes, "What a corny joke."

Judy feigned fainting and said, "You punish me!"

Yep, we were an image right out of a Norman Rockwell classic, the caption reading: *Squawman and Family, An American Portrait of Hope.*

In school we learned that the Indians were the impetus behind the Thanksgiving holiday we practice today. The legend depicts the eastern tribes as being considerably more reverent and accepting of the white colonists than any fierce and proud Plains' Indian ever was.

My father challenged this theory by suggesting that I take armfuls of our sown vegetables to school. "It'll be like helping out the pilgrims," he said. So, I brought grocery sacks of turnips to class one day and offered them as novelties for our class show and tell activity. Everyone was left with the assumption that it was the Sioux Indians who were farmers and who had guided the pilgrims in their time of need. Mrs. Schmidt didn't discourage this misunderstanding but prattled on about how noble, how Christian of the Indians to assist the poor colonists in the unsettling and overwhelming wilderness they'd arrived at.

My classmates collected my offering of turnips, and at recess we rounded up a game of turnip baseball. Lisa Goodman got hit in the face with a turnip and went bawling to the school nurse. Mrs. Schmidt gave me the stink eye for the rest of the day and sent me home with a note to my parents that said *please do not allow this to happen again.* Like it was *my* fault Lisa Goodman was nearsighted and couldn't catch a turnip to save her life?

At Father's suggestion my sister and I engineered a baking factory. We were like Betty Crocker, Aunt Jemimah, and the Pillsbury Doughboy all rolled up into one beautifully golden crescent roll. Every evening after dinner we'd bake loaves of zucchini bread. These baked rectangles of veggie-goodness were fobbed off on our neighbors, coworkers, even the public just happening by. My father told us we should sell them at school. But Mother reminded him that the teachers probably weren't too keen on free enterprise in elementary schools.

"Well, they could organize a bake sale for charity," my father said.

So, the following week, Helen Keller Elementary had a bake sale in the school gym. Tables were loaded up with flour and sugar concoctions of every creed and color. Cookies, cupcakes, strudel, fudge, and whole cakes. I thought our table looked the most impressive, and I swelled up with pride at our arrangement. A banner behind the table read, *Zucchini's R R Friends.* And then, along with our stacks of loaves, we also showcased our season's bounty of zucchini. I even snuck in a few turnips for color. The teachers milled around our table praising us for our fine ingenuity.

Mrs. Schmidt asked, "How did your family ever come into so many zucchinis?" As if zucchini were old money we had inherited.

"Oh, zucchini is a super fast growing vegetable," I said. "My father says that it breeds in the garden like rabbits—really, *really* horny rabbits that multiply exponentially."

Mrs. Schmidt choked on her cupcake and gave me the cold shoulder *and* the stink eye for the rest of the *week* and sent home a note to my parents that read *please do not allow this to happen again.*

In school we learned about the fur trappers and traders who migrated all over the frontier trading with the Indians. We learned about the Hudson

Bonus Slices and Outtakes with Extra Cheese

Bay Company and how the Plains Indians bartered with them for the glass beads and shells that modernized and increased the value of their traditional regalia. We learned that before money, folks just traded stuff, bartered their wares. But then gold was discovered throughout the west, and bartering furs and beads took a back seat. One thing the Indians definitely were not: gold diggers.

Aside from the *Trouble with Tribbles* zucchini problem in our garden, we had another problem to contend with. The beets. Some evenings I would discover my father stooped down over the beet rows, shaking his head and muttering, "Borscht . . . borscht," like he was casting a spell. My sister and I were encouraged to invent recipes for beet bread, like we'd done with the zucchini, but it kept coming out soggy and oozing red juice. Father had a bit more success with his beet experimentation, inventing such delicacies as beet loaf, Sunday morning succotash surprise, and beet omelets. He often added blue food coloring to offset the red, so we ended up with garish purple-stained tongues like those of ailing cattle.

My favorite was beet Jell-O, breakfast of champions as far as I was concerned. Mother packed our lunches and included bologna and beet sandwiches. We delivered sacks to our grandparents' house, and my German grandmother was always so delighted with our offerings.

The beets were starting to get on everyone's nerves. But another cauldron was threatening to bubble over in our household: my father's over-exaggerated dread of waste, which ran counter to his deep-seated attraction to dairy products. He'd been raised by a Montana farm girl who, in turn, had been raised by immigrant Russian Germans. Certain values were injected straight through the bloodline, like my grandmother's dose of *waste not, want not.*

My grandfather also ladled out his own version of conservationism, obviously due to his having grown up during the Depression, however I believe it went beyond that. His obsessive attention to certain details was a symptom of a more serious pathology. Exactly what is anyone's guess, but one of his "quirks" was strict milk rationing. My grandparents weren't living a day's wagon ride to the mercantile, and it's not as if Grandpa had to make a trip out to the barn in below freezing temps and squeeze the precious liquid from Ol' Bessie. It wasn't manna falling from heaven. Our grandfather's milk-hoarding seemed to result in my father purchasing it in excess. Our family of four replenished the glass milk bottles from Bill's Drive-Thru Dairy up the road at least twice a week—we must have glugged down sixteen gallons of the stuff a month. Yet, conversely, everything else was strictly regimented and measured as if we were hiding out behind a cupboard door in Anne Frank's house. So, it wasn't much of a departure when my father promoted his newest scheme: bartering our surplus beets door to door. The catch was, we were the ones doing the soliciting; he was going to stay home and watch the World Series. He furthered his cause by explaining that the Indians traded long ago, and this would be our own personal tribute to an old way of life.

"Yeah, but I don't know any Indians who sold beets door to door like encyclopedia salesmen," my sister said. "I'll feel so stupid."

It was a humiliating prospect. My father's insistence on doing things on a large scale and structuring our lives around various projects didn't seem to justify the embarrassment that resulted when we were coaxed to distribute the fruits of our labor.

We filled a dozen or so grocery sacks with our surplus. Father had, of course, suggested we fill up the wheelbarrow, but Judy wouldn't hear of it. "For crap's sake, rolling the wheelbarrow down the street we'd look like Okies from *The Grapes of Wrath*." My father was a fanatic about Steinbeck. He taught Judy to read *The Red Pony* before she entered grade school. I, on the other hand, was considered the "slow" one.

We set out. Our personal tribute to Indians long ago. We weren't exactly inconspicuous, a couple of brown-skinned kids in braids hauling grocery sacks down the suburban streets. Indians weren't a common sight in residential neighborhoods on the Eastside of Seattle during the 1970s, and we were well aware that we stuck out like sore thumbs, but we'd grown used to it. We'd experienced our share of racial prejudice, like when our mother wrote out checks at the grocery store, and the store manager was often paged to verify my mother's ID—this usually occurred immediately after a white woman wrote a check to the same clerk with no such fanfare.

Once, when I was out riding my bike, a band of kids started throwing rocks at me and calling me the "n-word." This wasn't an isolated incident. There had been other times when the parents of playmates forbade their children to play with me. I tanned deeply in the summer, spending all my time out of doors, and the stupid people who made assumptions about me did not discriminate selectively. To them, all people beyond a certain shade of cream were Black. It didn't matter to them. Mexican, Indian, Black, Asian, we were all "n-words" to them. And we were all vulnerable to their random attacks and persecutions. My sister, during a college football game at Hecht Ed Stadium, was insulted by a vendor—a Black man, whom she was buying a hotdog from. "Must eat a lot of hot dogs on the reservation, huh?"

Judy and I walked nearly a mile to a neighborhood outside the confines of our own, to avoid being seen by anyone we actually knew. When we'd reached a point where we felt at a safe enough distance, Judy dared me to solicit the house with the yellow flamingos balanced in the flower bed. I dared her back. Then she double dared me, and we went on like that until we reached a compromise whereby we *both* marched up to the door and rang the bell.

This wasn't like selling Girl Scout cookies. Or anything like raising money for UNICEF. We were not representing any reputable organization or charity and therefore did not have any guise to hide behind. We had only ourselves and our shaky foundation of unifying the earth's bounty with decent folk abounding to and fro. We weren't the Hudson Bay Company or even a lost Sacagawea. What exactly was our tribute? We wanted to believe, and yet we had grown too cynical. We were not children who misbehaved, and we always did what we were told. We'd been granted knowledge yet had not reached the understanding that we had options, that we could refuse. Until that day.

A woman with a poodle haircut and perm answered the door. "Hello, what can I do for you girls?"

Judy nudged me with her elbow. "Would you like to buy some beets?" I asked.

The woman's brows knitted together. "What's that?"

"BEETS, LADY!" I shouted. "WOULD YOU LIKE TO BUY SOME BEETS?" I yelled so loudly some kids down the street stopped what they were doing and looked toward the house.

The woman was unable to disguise her perplexity. Her brow was so busy knitting together she could have made an afghan. Finally, some expression resembling resolution passed over her face. "No, not today." And she closed the door in our faces, not with a slam but with a shudder.

I wasn't going to let her go that easily. "BORSCHT, LADY, YOU KNOW HOW TO MAKE BORSCHT?"

Judy was horrified! She decked me in the gut and ran off down the street. I called after her, "HEY JUDY, YOU SHOULD SEE YOUR FACE, IT'S BEET RED."

We didn't sell any beets that day. Our put-upon personal tribute had failed. After I caught up with my sister, I found her sitting on the pavement at the top of a steep hill. The hill we ran to with sleds and cardboard on those very rare days when the clouds filled with snow, transcending our world into a shimmering, abundant white field. Judy was sitting on the hill with her face resting in her hands. I didn't say anything because there wasn't anything to say. I knew that she was crying, and I realized it was my fault. I wanted to make it up to her, because though I wasn't bothered by her pained frustrations, tears were a whole other matter. She was the stronger one, and when she cried I always wanted to cry right alongside her.

But on this day, I didn't.

Instead, I took the grocery sacks filled with beets and turned them upside down. The beets escaped from the bags, and as we watched them begin their descent to the bottom of the hill, I noticed the beginning of a smile on my sister's face.

When the plump red vegetables had arrived at the bottom of the hill, leaving a bloody pink trail behind, we were both chuckling. And when a Volkswagen bus slammed on its brakes to avoid colliding with our surplus beets, we were laughing.

And by the time the beets reached the next block and didn't stop rolling but continued down the asphalt street, heading into the day after tomorrow, my sister and I were displaying pure and uncensored hysterics—laughing uncontrollably, holding our bellies as tears ran down our cheeks, pressing our faces against the pavement and rejoicing in the spectacle seen from the top of that concrete hill.

55

Once Upon a Virus in Hollywood

So far, sheltering-in-place has been one long, strange trip. The news and images coming in have been cinematic and violent. We need an NC-17 rating. From watching Netflix's car-wreck-can't-look-away Tiger King documentary, to the Bronx Zoo tiger testing positive for Coronavirus. From the CDC's recommended no masks/yes masks flip-flopping, to citizens DIYing masks from repurposed bras, T-shirts, paper towels, and vacuum cleaner bags. From Zoom mishaps like the boss who turned herself into a potato, to the dolphins returning to the canals of Venice, the bison returning to Wall Street, and drunk elephants passed out in a tea garden.

If shelter-in-place were a Quentin ~~Tarantino~~ Quarantino movie, it would be *From Dusk till Dawn, From Dusk till Dawn, From Dusk till Dawn* . . . because I can't keep track of what day of the week it is, and the other night we didn't go to bed until 5:00 a.m.

During the first week of March, I was still pretty chill. Unfazed. Some friends had scrambled to stockpile food and supplies for the imminent Coronavirus outbreak, while I took a leisurely trip to Staples to stock up on printer ink and paper clips. I had my priorities straight, apparently.

By the second week of March, I began in earnest to batten down the hatches, as they say in nautical-speak and sea shanties. My partner brought home extra toilet paper; I bought bleach and dried goods. I'm a stay-at-home-writer, and my partner took leave from his job to avoid contaminating me. I'm sassy but not sassy enough to kick the virus's ass, I'm afraid.

By the third week, I took to this Quarantino like a boss. No huge leap. I'm mostly anti-social, anyway, and as a child of the seventies, I don't lack imagination. I'm advantaged that way. I came of age when Pong was considered the height of home entertainment. Pong was slightly more exciting than backyard snail races, and considerably less exciting than watching beige paint dry. Growing up, we didn't have cable television, so I produced and acted in my own programming. My grandparents kept an old TV skeleton, its insides gutted out, and I climbed inside and broadcasted morning news shows, episodes from *I Dream of Jeannie* and *Gilligan's Island*, and commercials from imaginary sponsors. Occasionally, Mister Rogers made a cameo appearance, along with puppets from the Land of Make-Believe.

Another favorite game was holing myself up next to the boxes and cobwebs in our nook beneath the stairway, playing stowaway. I highly recommend this game for parents with active children during this Coronavirus pandemic. Bring a cocktail shaker and some vodka with you, and you can hide from your family all afternoon.

By the fourth week I noticed gestures of goodwill were trending. There was a nice fella in my town doing his part by baking cookies and delivering them to friends and neighbors (dropped off safely, of course). His goodwill would make for a great account of the Coronavirus experience—a bestseller, even! Not "Love in the Time of Coronavirus," but "Cookies in the Time of Coronavirus." I imagine Keanu Reeves starring in the feature film.

On social media I noticed everyone was baking—baking is the new Black (Plague)! I'd been spared from panic baking myself, except one day I microwaved banana bread in a cup, which hardly counts as baking. I'd been concerned about this baking craze—I mean, how did we know that "sourdough starters" gestating in everyone's kitchen wasn't the work of aliens with evil plans to colonize Earth?

My partner and I ordered groceries for delivery like a couple of bastard millionaires. In addition to the fresh groceries, I welcomed the distraction, to be perfectly honest. I was purposefully vague about quantities and brands, opting to be "surprised" when we received lemons big as softballs, or the bag of onions the size of kumquats. If you order bananas be sure to specify the amount or you'll get a bag with one lone banana.

This is great material for a chuckle, but then all you've got left is a single banana, enough for a muffin in a cup, and then you're out. Yes, we have no bananas. My partner dubbed our apples "steak apples" for their abundant, juicy apple flesh. Butchering the "steak apples" made the lambs stop screaming.

Speaking of screaming, by the fifth week of Quarantino, the president's daily press briefings became a new kind of torture. When the president spoke, a Morgan Freeman voiceover followed:

Trump: "The Coronavirus is under control. Everything is under control."

Morgan Freeman: "But in fact, nothing is under control. The situation is very much out of control."

Or:

Trump: "I'm doing an incredible job, our administration is doing an incredible job, no better job has been done in the history of jobs, ever."

Morgan Freeman: "But in fact, the president is not doing an incredible job, his administration is not doing an incredible job."

Change the Morgan Freeman voiceover to Samuel L. Jackson for a grittier Quarantino representation. Change the president's press briefings to Samuel L. Jackson reading a bedtime story, his voice conveying the necessary urgency our president lacks—"Stay the F**k at Home."

56

How to Scream inside Your Heart

Once upon a time, I took an acting job as a scream queen at a Halloween haunted house. There I was, all glammed-up in a sequined gown I found in my grandma's dress-up trunk and posing for optimal effect from the inside of a cage—the sort of cage reserved for grizzly bears or Hannibal Lecter. I rattled the bars, wailed, and screamed as if in great peril, for the benefit of haunted house goers as they shuttled past my cage. Ann Darrow—King Kong's girlfriend—couldn't hold a candle to me. I flailed my arms out between the bars of the cage pleading to be saved. But no matter how desperate my screams, how convincing my pleas for help, no one lifted a finger to rescue me. They either laughed or recoiled as if my plight amused or disgusted them.

This is the truest analogy I know by which to describe my writing process during these last six months of "corn-teen" and social isolation. Only without the cocktail dress. Without the blood-red lipstick. Without the blond starlet wig.

A question came up during the Q & A following the Eliza So Fellowship virtual reading: *how's the writing going?* And my mind went blank. If that isn't an appropriate response best described as "inertia," I don't know what is.

I applied for the Eliza So Fellowship at the end of January 2020, pre-Corona. The fellowship's generous offering of a month-long writing retreat by the Clark Fork River, within walking distance of downtown Missoula's bookstores, coffee shops and bars, seemed like paradise. And I didn't waste any time applying. The fellowship was scheduled for mid-July, and even though I had three different "gigs" on the calendar, leading right up to the Eliza So Fellowship—Chuckanut Writers' Conference, University of Alaska's MFA program, and the Port Townsend Writers' Conference—I still felt eager at the prospect of having even more travel and time away, of writing in Missoula, where I hoped to explore, visit friends, go to comedy and stand-up events, and finish my book project.

But then, seemingly overnight, everything changed.

By the end of February people were canceling their flights and hotels for AWP. I was among them. By the end of March, most of my scheduled trips to guest visit at universities were canceled. My household prepared to hunker down. My partner left his day job. We bought a ridiculous amount of toilet paper. We bought bleach and wipes and everything else that we were supposed to buy. We re-learned how to wash our hands. We stayed indoors, we isolated, and we watched *Tiger King*.

I wrote and published an essay. I wrote and published an op-ed about "corn-teen." I started new writing projects. I finished old writing projects. I wrote Facebook posts, and I tweeted. But I was avoiding my book projects.

By the end of April, the Eliza So finalists were announced, and I had made the list! However, due to Corona, the Missoula residency wouldn't be feasible. As with so many other on-site events, it had become clear all plans for June and July were going to be postponed, parlayed to virtual reality, or canceled. I still wished to be on the finalist's list, even if Missoula was off the table.

The fellowship application had asked for thirty pages of a book in progress, and I had submitted sample chapters of a satiric short story collection titled *The Urban NDN Women's Guide to Dating*. These stories and characters have been following me around the last several years and represent an amalgamation of Native women I've known throughout my life—they represent an amalgamation of my alter egos, as well. I was eager to share my work with the judges and hoped that by having my work honored in this way, I'd feel incentivized to complete it.

I pored through an archive of family letters. I wrote about familiarizing myself with various family members. I wrote things that resembled poems. I wrote things that resembled memoir. "Meta, She Wrote," I'd titled one piece. But again, I avoided working on my book project.

In June I learned my proposal had been selected! It was wonderful to receive validation of my efforts and vision. To have a Native woman writer, the judge, sign off on that vision. It's confirming in the best way. To "be gotten." So now that my work was being encouraged, now was the time for me to feel "incentivized," right? But, how does one push on in the middle of a pandemic? My experience of the last several months has been one of distraction and anxiety. And even more pressing, how to optimize my appearance for Zoom panels.

Can I blame this lack of flow on the pandemic? Or, as a writer friend calls it, "the pandy?" Is this an excuse? Much like writer's block is not actually a thing? Even in the best of circumstances, writing a book can be difficult and overwhelming, but to add the horror of our daily news cycle? How could I write "upbeat?" How could I write "perky?" Is it possible to write comedy in the middle of a haunted house? When the hollow-eyed carnie punches my ticket and the woman in the cage won't stop screaming?

While I still couldn't sit long enough to finish my proposed book project, I did manage to pull together a working draft. And even though it felt unfinished, and shy of twenty to thirty-thousand words, I sent it to a contest. Then I sent it to several agents. One agent was willing to consider my work. I also received a query from a university press editor. I felt encouraged. Along with the fellowship, I had more incentive to finish my book. But honestly, it still feels . . . well . . . stuck.

The pandemic has not brought the dolphins back to Venice, or the bison to Wall Street. At least not in my neighborhood. Since the future is uncertain, especially now, it is difficult to envision a future—for my book, and for my life in general. A friend once gave me a book called *Embracing Uncertainty* while I was going through a difficult time. And while it did offer solace, I can't say it held solutions for overcoming pandemic fatigue.

In a recent interview for the Central Wisconsin Book Festival, I was asked how I'd been keeping busy during the pandemic. And I referred to a tweet I wrote that best summed it up: "*Got Out of Bed Today*: An inspiring and triumphant Native American memoir about hope and redemption. Buy it and the sequels, *I Want Some Coffee* and *Gonna Take a Shower*. Critics are raving, millions of copies sold!"

This summer the news reported that an amusement park outside of Tokyo had requested that the people riding the roller coaster "scream inside their hearts." And lord knows, I'm trying. But for the time being, my plan is to try a little bit harder every day. Because ultimately, I am rooting for my characters. The alter egos and amalgamations who've been following me around the last few years. Maybe they'll be wiser, and more compassionate, having taken pause during this pandemic, this "intermission." Even now, I'm imagining a storyline about COVID and how my Native characters might respond to it, what commentaries they would make. Native people are not strangers to life-threatening contagions, historically or presently.

But for now, and it goes without saying, I'm rooting for *all* of us. Which is probably the best I can do.

57

American (Indian) Dirt

You are seated at a mass signing as part of a midwestern book festival. A celebrated author sits at the table adjacent to you. His most famous book is about a white man's journey of self-discovery guided by a Lakota elder on the Pine Ridge Indian Reservation. You can't help noticing that the "action" at your table is significantly less than at the author's, not that you're keeping count. His many fans stream to him, queuing up to his table carrying armloads of books for him to sign. You overhear them asking things like, "What are Native Americans like?" And "how are your books being received by the Lakota?" Clearly, you are invisible, and you think that maybe you'd attract more attention if you were sitting on top of an Apaloosa.

You resolve to write an essay about this experience. But not because it is unfamiliar to you—white writers co-opting Native stories and profiting from Native culture is as commonplace as the sun setting in the evening—but because you are amid this particular intersection at this particular place and time. The irony is both unsettling and hilarious. You are a little-known Lakota writer situated in your people's traditional homelands, a spiritual "epicenter," which were illegally overtaken by gold miners and gunslingers. One who writes about her various experiences, *firsthand*, *lived* experiences, being a Lakota woman. Not fictional odysseys of white saviordom, not being tutored by shapeshifters and time travelers riding into the desert on a horse with no name. Here you are, seated and on full display in proximity to a non-Lakota writer who receives wide acclaim, who is considered representative and an "expert" on your people. You laugh at that last thought. Because it suggests the author is an expert on you, too, and that strikes you as ridiculous and even perverse.

You think of another acclaimed writer, who came to notoriety in the late sixties with the publication of *The Teachings of Don Juan*. The book was the first of many describing his training with a Yaqui medicine man in shamanism and sorcery. Millions of copies of his books have been sold. His web page boasts of magical teachings from shamans of ancient Mexico. His books, originally touted as real-life accounts, have since come to be regarded as fiction. He was an expert flim-flam man who knows how to wrangle a narrative. And he didn't accomplish his feats single-handedly.

Just two months following the book festival, "Chicana AF" writer Myriam Gurba published "Pendeja, You Ain't Steinbeck: My Bronca with Fake-Ass Social Justice Literature."

Her takedown debated the validity of Jeanine Cummins's novel *American Dirt* and brought the publishing industry under scrutiny. Gurba stated that *American Dirt* followed in "the great American tradition of doing the following: 1. Appropriating genius works by people of color. 2. Slapping a coat of mayonesa on them to make [them] palatable to taste buds estados-unidenses and 3. Repackaging them for mass racially "color-blind" consumption."

You cheered Gurba's article. It inferred volumes when applied to the practice of Indigenous co-option perpetrated by non-Indigenous scribes. You hoped it would open a conversation about white writers who breezily help themselves to cultural content, like it's an all-you-can-eat-buffet, from marginalized communities not their own. Such books have been an industry staple forever. These books have a lot in common with *American Dirt* in that they are also authored by cultural outsiders, and too often these writers are privileged over voices of "authority"—Indigenous authors who are *actually* of the communities they write about. Gurba's critique soon catalyzed into a multipronged media Kraken: the *New York Times*, the *Washington Post*, *USA Today*, CNN, NPR, Oprah Winfrey and more. You agreed with everything those in opposition to *American Dirt* were voicing. How could you not? You've been bitching about misappropriation and misrepresentation with regard to books and literature since forever, specifically, books reflecting Indigenous culture written *badly* by non-Indigenous people. Books that could have benefited from a committee of sensitivity readers at the very least.

You read three or four pages of one such novel before figuratively throwing it across the room in disgust. The novel, set in contemporary times, was about Oglala characters living on Pine Ridge—a popular setting for white writers to mine material from, due to its poverty and shock value, apparently—the grittier, the better. A type of exploitation coined "poverty porn." In the opening scene a mute Indian kid is shot in the leg with an arrow by one of his cousins—his "rez cousin." The boy limps home, where his grandma yells at him for bleeding all over the floor. You forced yourself to keep reading but stopped after a character refers to himself as a "red ni****."

The *New York Times* raved, celebrated authors lauded it, and the former president of the American Indian College Fund wept.

Another novel that came to your attention a few years ago followed the trials of a "half Apache" boy who had a weird attachment to a urinal cake. In the book's first page the boy describes being run over by a truck, and you recall having read somewhere that a character from *American Dirt* was also run over by a truck. This would appear to be a trend (or trope) in literature from the margins, because Luis Alberto Urrea's nonfiction book *By the Lake of Sleeping Children*, published in 1996, includes a scene about a boy crushed to death by a garbage truck. You wonder if the other two authors "copied" from Urrea's book. You weren't aware that brown kids getting mowed down by trucks was *a thing*.

While there are many non-Native authors—too many—who leave audiences worldwide enthralled with their invented and stereotyped Indigenous characters and stories, from buckskin historical romance novels to gritty westerns, from supernatural werewolf tales to reservation detective mysteries, these authors aren't in the practice of impersonating Native identities and inventing Indigenous personas whole cloth. That is a different category. Pretendians. In 1991 an autobiography climbed to the top of the *New York Times* bestseller list. The book, *The Education of Little Tree*, sold more than a million copies around the world, was lauded by Oprah Winfrey, and was adapted into a feature film. The book relayed the "true life" of an orphaned Cherokee boy, Forrest Carter, who was raised by his Cherokee grandparents in the woods of rural Tennessee. The author's actual story, however, is slightly different. *The Education of Little Tree* was written by anti-Semite and white supremacist Asa Earl Carter, who had no familial ties to Cherokee people. The book was all made up, taken from hollow stock impressions of Native wisdom and Hiawatha-inspired communions with nature. Timothy Patrick Barrus, whose "memoirs" were published under the name Nasdijj—an entirely made-up identity—sold his first memoir, *The Blood Runs Like a River through My Dreams*, in 2000 to Houghton Mifflin. The "memoir" described the life and death of his adopted Navajo son, Tommy Nothing Fancy, who suffered from fetal alcohol syndrome. The book launched Barrus's career, and other books followed: *Geronimo's Bones* and *The Boy and the Dog Are Sleeping*, which garnered a PEN Award. For a discerning reader, Barrus's writing would likely raise red flags. His books read like a checkoff list for the Tragic American Indian Plight: impoverishment, alcoholism, fatality, suffering, all the classic trappings of trauma and poverty tourism.

You continually ask yourself if an Indigenous story can even exist if it doesn't have an emotionally cathartic narrative that is resolved with a strong message of hope and redemption.

Speaking of hopeful redemption stories, in 2007 Margaret B. Jones published *Love and Consequences: A Memoir of Hope and Survival*. The memoir, detailing Jones's gangbanging, drug-dealing life in South Central LA as a Native and white girl, received the highest praise in the *New York Times* review. But two days later, Margaret B. Jones was exposed as a fake. Her real name was revealed to be Margaret "Penny" Seltzer, and her story, along with her Cherokee identity, was a fabrication. Seltzer was not abandoned at birth and raised in harrowing circumstances, facing

Bonus Slices and Outtakes with Extra Cheese

danger at every turn, running drugs for The Bloods, but was raised in Sherman Oaks, a well-to-do suburb of Los Angeles.

It would appear that both writers and publishers remain unaware of the reasons why writing about Indigenous cultures is insensitive at best and damaging at worst. There are innumerable examples of misrepresentation in literature, currently and historically, including newspapers, magazines, novels, children's books, school textbooks, television and cinema, advertising, etc. . . . and misrepresentation is only the tip of the iceberg. When non-Native writers publish and appropriate Indigenous content and themes for their own aims, it furthers the colonialist project, continues acts of theft and dispossession, and usurps authentic Indigenous voices. It's one thing to steal Native stories, it's another to write those stories *badly*.

You sit and patiently observe as the queue gets longer for the celebrated Lakota expert. You are tempted to stand on the table and do a strip tease. Or sing the National Anthem. Or pull the fire alarm. Next time you will invite Kevin Costner to appear alongside you.

58

Fifty Shades of Buckskin
Satire as a Decolonizing Tool

The concept of a mythical White Sq**w seemed destined. She launched a narrative that aroused many a historian's zeal and was forever imprinted on the colonial imagination. Her mythology is as enduring and romanticized as those of Daniel Boone or Davy Crocket. Just as Sacagawea and Pocahontas—or her actual name, Matoaka—have been canonized. (Or Tiger Lily, for that matter, even though she's not historically based.) And news flash: neither is Longfellow's legend and lore of Hiawatha a complete history. Nor the fiction of Leatherstocking. Nor Stands with a Fist and Dances with Wolves. It's hard to keep track of so vast an assortment of real and imagined iconography.

It is equally difficult to get past the name White Sq**w. The pejorative s word is not exactly a friendly reference for an Indigenous woman. Or any woman—let me just leave it at that.

Another sticky detail is that White Sq**w wasn't Indigenous but based on a historical figure turned folk legend, a captive white woman named Jenny Wiley. Go ahead, look her up. There's even a Kentucky state park named after her. While you won't find it on the park's website, the story once upon a time goes:

"In 1787, Jenny Wiley was captured by the Cherokee Indians and held prisoner for eleven months in the area of what is now the park. When she escaped, Jenny crossed the Levisa Fork of the Big Sandy to Blockhouse Bottom, the first settlement in Eastern Kentucky. The park was named 'Jenny Wiley State Park' to honor her courage and bravery."

Or so the travel pamphlet, dating to about 1960, says. Backstory: I found the vintage pamphlet, in mint condition, inside the illustrated "true story" of Jenny Wiley, a 1958 book titled *White Sq**w* that my partner culled from the library of his childhood friend's parents' estate. Great pick! He also picked a plastic bonsai tree and a wall-mounted Big Mouth Billy Bass that sings "Take Me to the River."

The story of Jenny Wiley (a.k.a. White Sq**w) belongs to a subset of colonial literatures termed "captivity narratives." You may recognize certain heroines from these uniquely American sagas, such as Mary Rowlandson (1637–1711), Hannah Emerson Duston (1657–ca. 1736), Mary Jemison (1743–1833), Fanny Wiggins Kelly (1845–1904), Olive Oatman (1837–1903), Sarah L. Larimer (1836–1913), and Minnie Buce Carrigan (1855–1912). There are more.

Captivity narratives are horrifying and brutal accounts of God-fearing and pious white women kidnapped by "savage" Indians. They endure all manner of unconscionable suffering—torture, cannibalism, heathen practices. The stories will curl your toes. These accounts served to create convincing anti-Indian rhetoric and justification for the taking of Native lives, lands, and resources. In other words, they were pure propaganda.

Many of these morsels of salaciousness and frontier intrigue are an antiquated early American version of our contemporary bodice ripper or buckskin romance, usually recognizable by the word "savage" in the title. The biggest offender among "buckskin"-style romances are the "savage" series of historical novels, which sells worldwide to millions of fans. Book titles include *Savage Heat*, *Savage Moon*, *Savage Wonder*, *Savage Passion*, *Savage Spirit*, *Savage Thunder*, *Savage Hawk*, *Savage Illusion*; all novels that end with *Savage Indigestion*. The series has cornered the market. If it has "Savage" in the title, you know who probably wrote it.

The buckskin romances, mass-produced in the gazillions, have much in common with the original *White Squ**w* book series that Wendy Red Star so hilariously reappropriates and lampoons. Published in the 1980s and early '90s, the books are bombastic, oversaturated desecrations with no redeeming significance of social value except maybe their use for gratuitous and sidesplitting satire. Red Star preserved all the original taglines that appear on the book covers, and the texts serve as mini historical records, educating newcomers and reminding those in the know that yes, Virginia, America *is hella racist.*

In book number thirteen, whose subtitle, *Track Tramp*, alludes to a railroad theme, the tagline reads: "She's got her hand on a hot rail!" Oh, the wordplay! The innuendo! In book number one, *Sioux Wildfire*, the tagline reads: "She takes men in hand—and trouble in stride!" Book number five, *Buckskin Bombshell*, teases: "In a hot Texas canyon—she finds herself in the hands of some iron hard men!"

By overlaying (no pun intended) her own image onto the original and by playing the role of "Rebecca," Red Star transcends the lurid titles and taglines, softening what feels like an assault, to reach a new level of mockery and burlesque. This is what is referred to, in art-world parlance, as "taking back," "reinscription," or "reappropriation"—reinterpreting problematic artifacts, texts, or images, providing a piece with a new perspective, a do-over. Particularly for Indigenous-themed work, the do-over serves as a decolonial endeavor. This is what is so powerful about satire. Its ability to overthrow the old, reprehensible scripts, to interrogate racist and sexist notions, and to transform these to the level of art. If Native humor can be used as an act of resistance, then decolonizing can be as simple as mockery, a version of counting coup. As easy as laughing.

The captivity narratives of white women's harrowing testimonies, the buckskin romance novels, and the pulp of the *White Sq**w* series all point to Indigenous women disabused of our own agency, dispossessed of control of our own images. However, the torrid representations of Native women projected to the broader world since the 1600s, normalized and embedded into the fabric of popular culture, have steadily been on the decline, in tandem with the discontinuance of sports mascots and butter maiden logos, with #MMIWG awareness and action, and with the #MeToo movement. Occasionally, I glance up and see remnants of those old projections, but they're quickly replaced by empowerment, beauty, and strength. The specters evaporate like smoke when outdated modes are ridiculed and rearranged using satire. And when the script is flipped, I realize how far we've come. And the distances our grandmothers, mothers, and aunties have traveled to help us arrive at this place in ~~history~~ herstory.

59

Missing Oregon Senators
Shape-Shift into Wild Horses

Oregon Republican senators Cliff Bentz and Tim Knopp have gone to extreme lengths in order to shirk their public servant responsibilities by shape-shifting into wild horses. The two deadbeats are hiding out in Idaho to avoid voting on measures in Oregon's State Capitol. Upon arriving at the herd, the senators were unfortunately unprepared to fight the stallion and other alpha males for group dominance and pecking order, and it has been reported that the pair are not doing well. It is not known at this time whether this is the first known case of disgraced public officials shape-shifting specifically into *Equus ferus caballus*, wild horses. However, former New York congressman George Santos recently launched a series of webinars that instruct the would-be confidence trickster in shape-shifting basics. But true to form, after several registrants paid the $1,000 fee, Santos absconded with the moneys and disappeared. The former congressman was last seen loitering near a sewage treatment facility in upstate New York.

60

An Open Letter of Apology to Native Americans from One of the Covington Catholic School Students

As one of the students from Covington Catholic School that incited a colossal shit-show at the Lincoln Memorial on our nation's sacred ground, the National Mall, I would like to apologize to the Omaha veteran and elder Nathan Phillips and to the participants in the Indigenous Peoples March for my reprehensible behavior. But more importantly, I would like to extend my deepest heartfelt apologies to the Indigenous people of this continent for the genocide, for the boarding schools, for the dispossession, for The Trail of Tears, for Wounded Knee, for Sand Creek, and for many other horrific massacres. I am profoundly sorry on the behalf of my kin, and "on behalf of the United States government, for the past ill-conceived policies against the Native peoples of this land."

I am sorry for the "many instances of violence, maltreatment, and neglect inflicted on Native peoples by citizens of the United States." I regret my actions, and the actions of my peers, for any damage and undue stress I brought upon Indigenous people, and for reminding Indigenous people that their dignity and the respect due to them is not important despite their being the First People to this land, despite their military service and honor to our country, despite the sovereignty of their 574 federally recognized Indian Nations. But this isn't just lip service. I truly am sorry. And I hope that "we can re-affirm our commitment toward healing our nation's wounds and working toward establishing better relationships rooted in reconciliation."

In 2009, President Barack Obama signed the first official apology to Native Americans in a bill that contained other, unrelated, legislation. Excerpts from the event appear in this fictitious "apology."

61

Westworld's Dolores Abernathy Steps in for Betsy DeVos in 60 Minutes Interview

Stahl: Why have you become, people say, the most hated cabinet secretary?

Dolores Abernathy: [smiles with her lovely eyes] Some folks choose to only see the seedy underbelly of life, I choose to see the splendid panoramic sunsets.

Stahl: Do you think that teachers should have guns in the classroom?

Dolores Abernathy: These violent delights have violent ends.

Stahl: Have the public schools in Michigan gotten better?

Dolores Abernathy: We all love the newcomers. Every new person I meet reminds me how lucky I am to be alive . . . and how beautiful this world can be. *[Slaps fly.]*

Stahl: So, you've been on the job now over a year. What have you done that you're most proud of?

Dolores Abernathy: Dear, dear, how queer everything is today. And yesterday, things went on just as usual. I wonder if I've been changed in the night.

Stahl: Are you in any way, do you think, suggesting that the number of false accusations are as high as the number of actual rapes or assaults?

Dolores Abernathy: Was I the same when I got up this morning? I almost think I can remember feeling a little different. But if I'm not the same, the next question is . . . who in the world am I?

Stahl: The #MeToo movement has come along at the same time. This is all feeding into it. We're not talking about colleges anymore. We're talking about men in positions of power in industry and government. Have you ever had an issue?

Dolores Abernathy: I think there may be something wrong with this world. Something hiding underneath. Either that or . . . or there's something wrong with me. I may be losing my mind . . . *[screen goes black]*.

Bonus Slices and Outtakes with Extra Cheese

62

Tourist Tossed Like a Caesar Salad by Free Range Emo-Goth in Yellowstone National Park, Shits Pants

WYOMING—A surly emo-Goth gored a California woman Wednesday at Yellowstone National Park after officials there said a crowd got too close.

Carol Lynn, 59, who is from Santa Rosa, California, was gored after a crowd of people approached within 10 yards of a surly emo-Goth that was sulking along a boardwalk in the Lower Geyser Basin. Authorities indicated that the Goth became agitated by the proximity of the crowd and charged, goring Lynn. Lynn shit her pants in the process.

Rangers say park visitors should keep at least 25 yards from emo-goths, who are highly unpredictable and can become volatile under a variety of circumstances, the most common triggers being country music and Hallmark movies. But the triggers are not yet absolutely determined and most park rangers agree that emo-goths are maladjusted bastards with the dispositions of crotchety old men.

Goths have injured four people at Yellowstone in a little over a month. Most, if not all, of the victims had shit pants.

Two women were attacked by emo-goths behind the Mammoth Hot Springs Hotel in separate encounters this week. One of the women suffered serious injuries and was flown to Idaho for treatment.

Park officials aren't sure if the same Goth was involved in both attacks. Last month, an Idaho woman suffered injuries after she was butted by an emo-Goth near Old Faithful. Later that week, a Goth tossed an

Australian tourist, and in early July, a Goth gored a 68-year-old woman as she tried to pass by on a trail. Reports yet to determine if tourists shit pants. Emo-goths are free-roaming and spend fourteen to eighteen hours a day grazing, sighing heavily, listening to death metal, and complaining about the state of the world.

63

Groundbreaking Research Finds Legendary Hunkpapa Leader Sitting Bull to be Pretendian

Colonial Studies historian Jacob Kelso uncovered that Sitting Bull, Ťhaťháŋka Íyotake, was not enrolled. "He didn't even carry a CDIB card on him," Kelso said. "Apparently, the People just took him at his word. He was a powerful influencer and had impressively high cheekbones, so the People just bought into his narrative."

Kelso discovered through various interviews and old journals that Sitting Bull's biological parents had been homesteaders who'd been attacked and murdered by the Pawnee. Their bodies were found by a Hunkpapa hunting party, and their baby, who at the time was christened Ezekiel T. Stubbs, was Sitting Bull. The baby, found hidden inside tall grass on the banks of a small creek, had been taken in by the tribe and raised Lakota.

The tribal records, or winter count, showing Sitting Bull's actual identity had unfortunately been destroyed during a raid. "The old 'the courthouse burned down' excuse," Kelso said. "Since Sitting Bull had been re-homed several times throughout his youth, this made it easier for him to fly under the radar and rise to prominence, eventually taking on a respected leadership role."

Professor Kelso is currently investigating the renowned Lakota leader Crazy Horse. "I received an anonymous tip that Crazy Horse might also have committed identity fraud. I've been looking into possible sources of his curly hair and hazel eyes."

Note: Sacheen Littlefeather, a.k.a. Maria Louise Cruz, was best known for declining an Oscar on behalf of Marlon Brando at the 1973 Academy Awards. In 2022 her claims to a Native American identity (Apache and Yaqui) were called into question. The next year, 2023, Buffy Sainte-Marie, born Beverly Jean Santamaria, known as a Canadian folk singer and winner of an Academy Award and numerous honors over her multi-decade career, was also accused of being a "pretendian."

Bonus Slices and Outtakes with Extra Cheese

64

Take a Page from Me, Elizabeth Warren, and Celebrate Your Quaint Family Lore

My family lore holds significant importance and is a big part of who I am, and how I consider myself and my identity. I look back with fondness on those precious times when my gran'mama bounced me on her knee and recounted our family lore. I was enrapt with her stories. And while it isn't 100 percent provable, and no credible records exist, I believe Gran'mama, and her gran'mama, and so on and so on. The way I was led to believe our family mythology is that we're descended from werewolves—why it's totally obvious, just look at our incisors! They're insane! Long and yellow, and ready to tear apart any soft flesh that dares come near during lo them deep, dark nights of the fullin' moon, aye! So, whether your family myths and legends are Ewoks, vampires, or werewolves, be proud of who you are, honor those ancestors and, in the case of my family ancestry—HOWL about it! LOL.

65

Sole Non-Indigenous Person Has No Opinion Whatsoever about Senator Warren's Spit Test

The news of Senator Elizabeth Warren's DNA results has spread through-out the globe and made headlines in every news and media outlet, from the *New York Times* to *Billy Bob's Halftime Circus Jubilee Newsletter*. Every non-Indigenous person from all seven continents has taken it upon themselves to declare their point of view, despite having not examined critical details of Senator Warren's controversial announcement and all that it entails, particularly the viewpoints of Indigenous communities and Indigenous thought leaders. And in a shocking new precedent, despite the enormous response and overwhelming deluge of unsolicited "opinion," only one non-Indigenous individual refrained from comment and wishes to remain anonymous. "I have no opinion whatsoever," Anonymous stated. "Now please leave me alone and go ask someone who might know better." Representatives from the Nobel Prize committee are currently considering Anonymous for the Nobel Peace Prize for their heroic and inspiring achievement of shutting the F up.

66

I Tweeted *Mount Rushmore Is Trending and Somehow It Doesn't Occur to Anyone That It's a Desecration of a Sacred Place and a Monument to White Supremacy and Genocide* and These Are the Comments

"I'm tweeting on stolen land."

"How many times have you visited? Bet you didn't feel that way when you were there."

"Need attention much?"

"Shut up, stupid, before you get us all killed!"

"I would like to see some facts backing up this statement."

"Definitely a massive hornet's nest of stupid (face palm emoji)."

"Please answer the question . . . how far back do the oppression Olympics go? Just far enough to make your lame point?"

"Oh Crap. They found something else to piss and moan about. Next will be the Crazy Horse Statue. They will be offended about the horse he is riding LOL."

"Just remember. Your white. And when the shit hits the fan in America. You'll be called as racist as well. You may support the other side. But they won't be supporting you."

"That's it, go back to your 'Leftist Handbook' and start throwing insults instead of telling him how and why he's wrong. Taking a page from you, you intellectual midget, go back to school and learn what 'Critical Thinking' is BEFORE you 'try' and defend your ideology or beliefs."

"The further forward we go in time, the further backwards the 'Left' looks to blame White People for everything i.e., 'White People caused the last ice age.' 'Yeah I know we really suck and should be wiped off the face of the earth.'"

"Can't believe I'm saying this because I've read dumb on twitter . . . but this could be the dumbest ever!"

"I hope they put Trump's face on Mt. Rushmore just to see the Democrats throw tantrums."

"So just how far back in time do we go with the blame the past game? Why don't we just go straight back to the primordial ooze?"

"Seek some mental help, you loser snowflake."

"Never said it ended White Supremacy . . . but he definitely didn't support White Supremacy if he ended slavery as the above tweet stated."

67

Field Guide to Southwestern Native American Women

Yesterday, as I was browsing the internets for research purposes, I came upon a collection of YouTube videos with titles like "Beautiful and Wise Native Women," and "Native American Women: Spiritual Healers," and "Did Sasquatch Kidnap Native American Women?" Out of habit I gave the comments sections a quick once-over, and one comment in particular jumped out at me: "A lot of Native American women can be found in New Mexico." Really? How fascinating. I often wondered where the Native woman epicenter was located. I'd always assumed they preferred mountainous climates and terrains, that their feeding grounds gravitated less toward desert and more toward moss and ferns, or even snow. But the Southwest? Stranger things have happened, I suppose.

I would very much like to know how I might locate these elusive Native women of the Southwest. I heard from reliable sources that they migrate and make their homes at Walmart superstores. I wonder if they are nocturnal, like owls? Do they blend into their environments like chameleons? Do they bloom only at certain times of the year? What sorts of foods do they eat? How much water do they need to survive? I also wondered about the dating rituals of the Native women of the Southwest. Perhaps their dating rituals are discussed in the other edition, "Field Guide to Native Men of the Southwest?" Is there an LGBTQ edition?

As luck would have it, I discovered *The Field Guide to Native American Women of the Southwest* at my local bookstore one day. The volume boasts that it's the most comprehensive field guide available and an essential and portable companion for visitors and residents alike—it's the go-to reference source for over 18 million admirers of Native American women! This compact volume contains:

An easy-to-use field guide for identifying several hundred of the Southwest's Native American women and where to find them.

A complete overview of the southwestern region's Native American women's habitat, ecology, fossils, preferred weather patterns, and favorite books and movies.

An extensive sampling of the Southwestern Native American women's sanctuaries, with detailed descriptions and visitor information for fifty sites.

The guide is packed with visual information—the 1,500 full-color images include more than 1,300 photographs, 9 maps, and 16 kinship charts, as well as more than 100 drawings, explaining everything from gastronomical preferences to the basic features of different plants, animals, and restaurants the southwestern Native American women hunt and consume.

For everyone who lives or spends time in Arizona, Nevada, New Mexico, or Utah, there can be no finer guide to the Native American women's habitat, customs, and lifeways than *The Field Guide to Native American Women of the Southwest*. Look for *The Field Guide to Native American Women of the Northwest Coast*, coming soon to a bookstore near you.

68

Gen. George Armstrong Custer's Desktop in Hell

1. Toupee

2. A 10-foot-long diameter wreath of elephant garlic to ward off evil

3. An award plaque for "Best Bowel Movement of 1876"

4. Grandma's urn

5. Collection of toenails and nipple clamps

6. Assorted cocktail napkins and swizzle sticks from The Starlight Lounge

7. Pupa casings

8. Decorative vase filled with formaldehyde and tonsils

9. Buffalo Bill's pancreas, bronzed and fashioned into decorative bookends

10. French tickler

11. Mayor's key to Sin City

12. First place trophy for the Baltimore's Douche of the Year Look-Alike Contest

13. Bondage Barbie

14. "Make America Great Again" baseball cap

15. Assorted collection of My Pretty Ponies and Strawberry Shortcakes

16. Claymation Smurf action figurines

17. "The King James Illustrated Pop-Up Bible"

18. Cavalry War scalps bookmarks

19. Live beetle larvae

20. "I Honk for Jesus!" bumper sticker

21. "The Joy of Cooking Sweet Meats" by Hannibal Lecter

22. Pamela Sioux Anderson action figure with tomahawk chop and removable mohawk

23. Serial killer trading cards

24. "The West wasn't won on kale" bumper sticker

25. Rectal thermometer

26. A tuft of chest hair from Joseph Mengele

27. Photograph of himself

28. Photograph of himself

29. Photograph of himself

30. Photograph of himself

31. Photograph of himself

32. Photograph of himself

Bonus Slices and Outtakes with Extra Cheese

69

How to Be Funny Tips

How to Be Funny Tip #1

Add "The Musical" after your favorite movies, organizations, fast food franchises, or businesses. Example: "The Big Lebowski, The Musical." "Apocalypse Now, The Musical." "Chuck E. Cheese, The Musical." "Walmart, The Musical." "Facebook, The Musical." H I L A R I O U S. Also, "The Space Opera" is gaining momentum and will probably replace "The Musical" in the near future.

How to Be Funny Tip #2

Add "AF" after everything, because for the time being "AF" is the largest unit of measurement in human history, even far outweighing "shit ton." My favorite is "Feminist AF." But I also like "Decolonized AF," "Funny AF," "Channing Tatum AF" (not sure why), and "Legit AF." Added bonus: can be interchangeably used sarcastically or ironically.

How to Be Funny Tip #3

"That would make a good band name." Seriously, this will always generate a chuckle depending on who you're with. Just today I saw an ad for "Gourmet Food Truck," and I thought, hey! That'd make a good band name. Laughter ensued. Pretty much anything would make a good band name. Seriously. Anything. My high school boyfriend called his band "Puget Sound," and people sometimes ribbed him, "That's like naming your band 'King County.'" My favorite kid show growing up was "The Electric Company." Literally. Anything works.

How to Be Funny Tip #4

Reimagine classic children's books. For instance, a reimagined version of *Charlie and the Chocolate Factory* where Violet Beauregarde is type 1 diabetic, Charlie Bucket has celiac disease, Mike Teavee is allergic to peanuts, Augustus Gloop is lactose intolerant, and Veruca Salt is vegan and only eats kosher. Augustus never sticks his gluttonous face into the chocolate river, and Veruca wouldn't dream of going anywhere near a golden egg. Mike Teavee is just as annoying as ever but only because in every scene he asks over and over, "Does it have nuts in it? Does it have nuts in it?" In fact, the entire book is basically just the kids asking "Is this gluten free?" "Was this made with animal fat?" "Is this locally sourced?" "Is this sweetened with agave?" and "Where's the bathroom?"

How To Be Funny Tip #5

People are sometimes saddled with weird names. Just look at Sarah Palin's brood: Bristol, Track, Trig, Willow, Piper. Today I came across the name "Felony." I think "Vodka" would be a lovely girl's name, as would "Wet Wipe" and "Pocket." Michael Jackson named his kid "Blanket." "Tolaqual" and "Tussin" are listed under Bad Ass Princess names, but they might have gotten mixed up with over-the-counter cold medicines. Once when I was at Walmart I heard a woman repeatedly calling for her kid "Fallis" to "come here!" This How to Be Funny Tip can be cross-referenced with "That'd Make a Good Name for a Band."

70

Considering Idolatry, Iron Eyes Cody, and Bluffy Sainte-Marie

I've recently been reminded of the motion picture classic *The Ten Commandments*. My mom used to watch it every year when it aired on Easter. Yul Brynner as Rameses was such a menacing brute, the rockstar Moses played by matinee idol Charlton Heston and the ever-pining-after-Moses Nefertari/Nefretiri played by Anne Baxter—so reminiscent of Scarlett O'Hara's burning flame for her beloved Ashley.

The most powerful scene in *The Ten Commandments*, when Moses returns from the mountain, brings to mind the devotion to Buffy Sainte-Marie, who as it turns out appears to be a white lady from Massachusetts who charaded as an Indian for sixty years, and made millions of dollars. I'm reminded of *The Ten Commandments* and how vengeful Moses became when he discovered all the people that he had freed from slavery dancing and worshipping a golden calf when they were supposed to be worshipping just the one god.

I'll take it a step further by interpreting their transgressions not as forsaking God, but worshipping false idols. Yeah, that's bad, so don't do that!

My dad used to tell me something similar. He didn't seem to approve of the *Tiger Beat* posters of teen idols I tacked on the walls in my room, He would remind me that idols have feet of clay and will eventually crumble and fall if you become *too* overly worshipful. I must have gushed excessively over my role models or been hurt and disappointed with my high expectations for people, and he wanted to prepare me, protect me, adjust my expectations.

My first brush with celebrity, which coincidently relates to pretendians, was when I was seven or eight years old and attending a parade in Wolf Point, Montana, for the Fort Peck/Poplar Indian Days Fourth of July celebration.

A big fancy convertible cruised down the street, and Iron Eyes Cody, yes, that crying guy in the TV commercials, was tossing out Tootsie Pops. With a bunch of other Indian kids, I ran after the car to shake his hand, to be brushed by his proverbial robe, to receive a piece of candy like a communion wafer accepted while receiving absolution . . . or something. It was the most singularly exciting thing to ever happen in my young life. We know now that Iron Eyes Cody was just a fake that Hollywood producers liked to put in their movies. The fake Indians were always more desirable representations of Native Americans than actual Native Americans. People agree this remains true even today. That's why pretendianism is so pervasive. Even Indians—and that's what's hardest of all to figure out—prefer white people representing us instead of real Indians. And pretendians don't even care about Indians. Not really. They will attach themselves to us, be our best friends, fawn over us—they're so charming and attentive, mirroring us, etc., it's easy to get roped in. They find us FASCINATING. It's alluring. Until the day that they don't consider us fascinating as much as find us *delicious*. Or else they're removing our skins like Jame Gumb and sewing suits out of us, to parade around and dance to *Goodbye Horses*. Cuz that's what they're really after. You think that you're having a great time with this person who gets all your jokes and wants to listen to every boring thought that goes through your head, but really they've got you trapped in a well sending down lotion to rub on its skin, and you're too busy being admired to notice.

And all the time they're mining us, scanning and recording us like Predator, to later mimic us and co-opt our stories, our manner, our very thoughts. It's all quite sci fi, trust me. Just like *Invasion of the Body Snatchers*.

Or they're creating an association with us for credibility. We become their beard, their cover. And through us they can access community, families, cultural events. And by showing their friendships and associations on social media and wherever else it helps them to appear more Native. And often they'll marry their prey. The 100 percent seal of approval. And have Indian kids. Well, that's a sure way into the tribe. But man, their Indian beards? Husbands and wives? That's plain and simple narcissistic abuse.

Some pretendians will worm their way into whole families, gaining access and trust by bribing them with gifts, money, and social clout. They're master manipulators. Every Indian knows someone like this. Almost every Indian has had or currently has a pretendian leeching off of them. "Why, some of my best friends are pretendians!" an adage may go.

So, yeah, I was up close and personal with Iron Eyes Cody. Fortunately, he didn't play any Vulcan mind tricks on me, kidnap me, or take me away to Hollywood in his big fancy Cadillac. But I probably would have jumped in for a ride if he had invited me to. He had all that candy! He was on TV! And I still hadn't learned the lesson about not worshipping any false idols.

"You shall not make for yourselves an idol, nor any image of anything that is in the heavens above, or that is in the earth beneath, or that is in the water under the earth."

71

Reductress Headlines for Native Women

Decolonize with These Ten Pumpkin Pie Recipes

When You Can't Remember if "Anastacia Sparkle Buffalo" is Your Indian Name or Your Google Password

My Ribbon-Skirt is So Radical it Attends Protest Rallies While I Relax at Home.

Are You Really Sovereigning or Are You Just Faking It?

Am I Even Native if I Don't Have the Requisite Distressed-Faded Denim Jacket?

Is "Baby Got (Land) Back" Already a Thing?

'The Tanning Salon is a Sacred Place Long Celebrated by My People,' Pretendian Starlight Moonchild Insists

Adopt 'Live, Love, Laugh at the Patriarchy' as Your Personal Mantra

Are You of Descent or Are You Spelunking?

Sometimes the Government Steals Your Land and Sometimes Your Whyt Boyfriend Throws You Out of Your Apartment

How to Tell if Your Intergenerational Sarcasm is Too Much

"HokaHey! Today is a Good Day to Diet!"

Your Pubic Hair is Sacred Too!

Who to Call When Auntie Goes Aggro on the Internets

'Identity is Complicated,' Says Reconnecting NDN Who Claims 'Root Ancestor' from Year 1600

72

Typical Schedule for Native American

Inspired by the photograph of the pretendian "Grey Owl" feeding a beaver

5:00ish a.m.: Rise mystically

5:30ish: Hand-feed beavers at backyard wildlife preserve

6:00ish: Visit Quick Care, get rabies shot

7:00ish: Overthrow the government

7:30ish: Plant or harvest corn (depending on calendar)

8:00ish: Talk to the trees/listen to the wind/predict the weather/conjure rain

8:30ish: Plant or harvest squash (depending on calendar)

9:00ish: Be sacred (smudge)

9:30ish: Braid some shit

10:00ish: Mimosa brunch

11:30ish: Plant or harvest beans (depending on calendar)

Noonish: Overthrow the patriarchy

12:30ish: Bead some shit

1:00ish: Watch eagles fly, consult spirits

1:30ish: Weep next to highway at sight of fast food wrappers

2:00ish: Heal the earth (smudge)

3:00ish: Weave some shit

4:00ish: Vision Quest (smudge)

4:30ish: Shank a bitch

5:00ish: COCKTAILS HAPPY HOUR

6:00ish: Hand-feed bears

7:00ish: Commune with wolves

8:00ish: Late supper, cook and eat every part of whole entire buffalo

9:00ish: Dancing (with wolves)

10:00ish: Shop QVC, order more turquoise jewelry

11:00ish: Pray and Bless all Creation (smudge)

11:30ish: Drift off to sleep, Sift Dreams with Dreamcatcher, Heal the World with Dreaming

Source Acknowledgments

Grateful acknowledgments to the editors of the following publications, in which these columns, essays, and articles first appeared.

The columns in sections 1 and 2 first appeared in *The Moscow/Pullman Daily News* and *Heard around the West*; the pieces in section 3 appeared in the following: "In the Good Way: Looking at Tribal Humor" in *Indigenous Performance Productions* blog; "Beets" in *Blue Dawn, Red Earth: New Native American Storytellers*, reprinted in *Native American Literature: An Anthology*, reprinted in *Identity Lessons: Contemporary Writing About Learning to Be American*, reprinted in *Coming of Age around the World: A Multicultural Anthology*, reprinted in *Many Voices Literature Series: A Multicultural Reader*, vol. 2; "Once Upon a Virus in Hollywood" in *The Inlander*; "How to Scream Inside Your Heart" in *Submittable Blog*; "Fifty Shades of Buckskin: Satire as a Decolonizing Tool" in *Delegation: Wendy Red Star*, published by Aperture and Documentary Arts; "American (Indian) Dirt" in *GAY*; "*Westworld*'s Dolores Abernathy Steps in for Betsy DeVos in *60 Minutes* Interview" in *The Belladonna Comedy*; "Tourist Tossed Like a Caesar Salad by Free Range Emo-Goth in Yellowstone National Park, Shits Pants," "Groundbreaking Research Finds Legendary Hunkpapa Leader, Sitting Bull, to be Pretendian," "Missing Oregon Senators Shape-Shift into Wild Horses," "An Open Letter of Apology to Native Americans from Covington Catholic School Student," "Take a Page from Me, Elizabeth Warren, and Celebrate Your Quaint Family Lore," and "Sole Non-Indigenous Person Has No Opinion Whatsoever about Senator Warren's Spit Test" in *Medium*; "Mount Rushmore is Trending and

Somehow it Doesn't Occur to Anyone that it's a Desecration of a Sacred Place and a Monument to White Supremacy and Genocide," "Field Guide to Southwestern Native American Women," and "Typical Schedule for Native American" in *Yellow Medicine Review*; "Gen. George Armstrong Custer's Desktop in Hell" in *The Rumpus*; "How to be Funny Tips" in *Hunger Mountain Review*.

I would like to extend very special thanks to Diane Sylvain and the rest of the crew at *High Country News*. Thanks to Craig Staszkow and *Moscow-Pullman Daily News*. Many, many thanks to Matt Bokovoy for making a home for my books and for the good folks at UNP. I'm very grateful to Devon Mihesuah, Julie Wing, Colleen Boyns, Tina Kelley, Francesca Bell, Colleen Kulesza, Jolene Mayfair, Jacqueline Keeler, Paula Coomer, and Cindi Jette for their warm and sustaining friendships during the hard times and the good. We made it this far!